STONE QUARRY WORKERS

SOCIAL SECURITY AND DEVELOPMENT ISSUES

STONE QUARRY WORKERS

SOCIAL SECURITY AND DEVELOPMENT ISSUES

By

Dr. ROBIN D. TRIBHUWAN

M.A., M.Sc. P.G.D.M., Ph.D.

&

JAYSHREE PATIL

M.A., M.Phil.

D P H

DISCOVERY PUBLISHING HOUSE PVT. LTD.

NEW DELHI-110 002

First Published-2009

ISBN 978-81-8356-427-4

Published by:

DISCOVERY PUBLISHING HOUSE PVT. LTD.

4831/24, Ansari Road, Prahlad Street
Darya Ganj, New Delhi-110002 (India)
Phone: 23279245 • Fax: 91-11-23253475
E-mail: dphbooks@rediffmail.com
dphtemp@indiatimes.com
web: www.discoverypublishinghouse.com

Printed at:

Sachin Printers
Delhi

PREFACE

Since the last three decades, Economists, Development Experts and Social Activists belonging to research, academic institutions and NGOs of National and International Caliber, have written and published several papers and books on unorganized sector. These scholars have evolved several theories in the concept of unorganized sector and problems of those labourers in this domain. While conducting review of secondary literature it was observed that there are hardly any Sociological studies on the above subject.

Although some of the European Sociologists did mention in their works, concepts such as haves and have not, division of labour, power structures and authority, problems of labourers, rights of labourers etc., one of the Sociologist who has precisely studied the labourers of informal sector as defined by him, gives a detail sociological account of the problems faced by brick-kiln workers, stone-quarry workers, sugarcane cutters, salt-pan workers and agricultural labourers in India. This Sociologist is none other than Jan Breman, a German Sociologist from University of Amsterdam, presented his Sociological views on labourers working in India's informal economy, in his book captioned, 'Footloose Labour'.

Besides Jan Breman's work, theoretical insights from Dr. Robin Tribhuwan and Ragnhild Andreassen's book Captioned

'Streets of Insecurity' which presents theoretical concepts of social insecurity among pavement dwellers of India, were studied. Studies by International Labour Organization and famous Social Scientists have also been referred to build up a strong theoretical base.

This piece of research is significant from social science point of view, because not many Sociologists and Anthropologists have worked intensively in this field. The main objective of this research is to explore the social, educational, economic, health, nutritional and environmental issues related to the livelihood of stone quarry communities. Due to time constraint, we could devote a year for collecting, analyzing and interpreting relevant data. However in the last chapter we have given areas of further research, which will certainly interest social scientists to take up in depth studies on various issues related to the life and development of the stone-quarry workers.

At the theoretical level this study will certainly be useful to researchers from Sociology, Anthropology, Economics, Political Science, Social work and Development Planning. At the more practical level, the study will certainly prove useful to policy makers and administrators to plan, implement, monitor and follow-up appropriate and culturally acceptable development programs and social security provisions for the poor and depressed stone-quarry workers of this country.

Dr. Robin D. Tribhuwan

Jayshree Patil

ACKNOWLEDGEMENTS

It gives us a great delight to place on record the valuable support and help given to us by certain individuals and organizations to complete this research work.

A special word of thanks to Mayuri Deshmukh, who helped us to take photographs of the stone quarry workers. We are grateful to Kiran Kurde and Mr. S.R. Kute for typing this book. A word of gratitude for Mr. and Mrs. Rege of 'Santulan' NGO in Pune for their guidance in the initial stages. Last but not the least we are thankful to all our respondents from the Laman, Wadar, Belder and Tirumal Communities, including others.

Dr. Robin D. Tribhuwan

Jayshree Patil

CONTENTS

Preface

Acknowledgements

1. **Introduction** 1

Social Security: Definition and Concepts
Definitions
Social Security and Legal Provisions: Indian Perspective
Social Security in Developing Countries
History of Social Security in India
Legal Provisions of Social Security
Review of Literature
Social Insecurity
Salient Features of Social Security
Analysis
Salient Features of Informal/Unorganized Sector
Profile of Stone Quarry Workers
Research Questions
Objectives of the Study
Significance of the Study

2. **Research Methodology** 30

Locale of the Study
Target Population
Method of Data Collection

Research Tools
Sampling Procedures
Analysis
Chapter Scheme

3. **Brief Ethnographic Profile of the Lamans, Wadars, Beldars and Tirumals** **33**
Ethnographic Profile of Lamans
Ethnographic Profile of Waders
Ethnographic Profile of Beldars
Ethnographic Profile of Tirumals

4. **Socio-economic Status of Stone Quarry Workers** **101**
Socio-economic Status of Target Population
Social Status
Educational Status
Economic Status
Children of Stone Quarry Workers
Discussions

5. **Health, Nutrition and Environmental Issues of Stone Quarry Workers** **162**
Health Policy: An Introduction
Health Issues of Stone Quarry Workers
Nutritional Issues of Stone Quarry Workers Children
Environmental Issues
Discussions

6. **Social Insecurity Among Stone Quarry Workers** **195**
Social Insecurity
Health Insecurity
Maternity Benefits
Nutritional Insecurity
Economic Insecurity
Civic Amenities
Benefit Received from Government Schemes

Availability of Documents
Caste wise Types of Documents Available
Educational Insecurity
Discussions
Social, Economic, Legal, Health, Nutritional Insecurities: Case Studies

7. **Summary of Findings, Conclusions and Recommendations** **213**
Summary
Findings
Conclusions
Recommendations

References ***234***

Index ***237***

1

INTRODUCTION

Since the last two decades the processes of development, modernisation and globalisation have invaded the rural areas as well as the psyche of the people. The process of rural-urban migration is rapidly taking place as a result of better employment opportunities in the metropolitan cities. The members of higher caste communities in the rural areas who have access to social, economic and political resources can afford to send their children for higher education and better job opportunities in the cities. With the partnership of foreign companies, corporate sector and IT Sector in the megacities of India have created job opportunities with higher scale of payment. These educated and economically well off rural youth are provided with internationally recognised social and economic security majors by the employer, company, corporate and IT Sector. Similarly, those rural youth who get into Government Sectors also get all the social security benefits.

Well, this is one side of the coin or scenario as regards the rural youth of educated adults who get recruited in organised sectors. Indian caste system, hierarchy has created several caste based occupational categories of labourers, artisans and workers who have never been part and parcel of an internationally acclaimed so called organised sector. With the process of rapid industrialisation, urbanisation, modernisation and technological development these unskilled, insecured, less empowered, socially stigmatised and depressed poor people find themselves unsecured in the mainstream of organised sector. This handicap of their socio-economic status and lack of professional skills has been a plus point of the shrud employers and small-scale entrepreneurs within and outskirts of the cities who have been successfully exploiting these labourers and workers of the unorganised sectors. In the process of this kind of exploitation the so-called labourers have been deprived of their social, economic and other rights as a workers of a company or an organisation for which they are working. This research study attempt to unveil the social insecurity among one such unorganised sector namely the stone-quarry and stone-crusher units. Before getting into the actual reality of social insecurity among the stone-quarry workers, it would be appropriate at this juncture to present certain theoretical concepts and definitions of terms such as unorganised sector, social security, informal sector and social insecurity by social scientists and more precisely by the sociologists.

SOCIAL SECURITY: DEFINITION AND CONCEPTS

At the international level, the International Labour Organisation, for the first time in 1986, recognised the need to address 'the question of how better to assist in all respect, the masses of the unorganised workers lacking adequate social protection'. Then in 1989, the ILO first proposed a comprehensive definition as follows:

"The protection which society provides for its members, through a series of public measures, against the economic and social distress that otherwise would be caused by the stoppage or substantial reduction in earnings resulting from sickness, maternity, employment injury, unemployment, invalidity, old age and death; the provision of medical care and the provisions of subsidies for families with children".

Most commentators agree that the ILO definition is inadequate for developing countries. The inadequacies are as follows:

1. It assumes that most persons are generally in a state of employment from which they can earn enough to meet their basic needs. In most developing countries, this view is unjustified;

2. It is true that most people work, but their work is intermittent, insecure and yields too little to cover the costs of social security;
3. Furthermore, often many of the components of social security are just not available to the workers at affordable prices;
4. The components of social security listed in the definition are based on the experiences of developed countries. Provision of food, for example, which is perhaps the most important component in developing countries, is not even mentioned in the list. (Subrahmanya and Jhabvala; 2000)

A number of alternative definitions have been suggested to overcome, the inadequacies of ILO definition.

DEFINITIONS

According to Subrahmanya, (1994) "Social security represents a guarantee, by the whole community to all its members, of the maintenance of their standard of living or at least of tolerable living conditions by means of redistribution of income based on National Solidarity. In other words, the concept of social security in its broadest sense should be understood to mean the support provided to the individual by the society to enable him/her to attain a reasonable standard of living, and to protect the same from falling due to the occurrence of any contingency." This definition stresses the obligation of society to maintain all its members in 'tolerable living conditions'.

According to I.P.Getubig, (1992) "Any kind of collective measures or activities designed to ensure that members of society meet their basic (such as adequate nutrition, shelter, health care and clean water supply), as well as being protected from contingencies (such as illness, disability, death, unemployment and old age), to enable them to maintain a standard of living consistent with social norms."

The definition of social security is further qualified by the 'protective' aspects of preventing a decline in living standards;

and 'promotive' aspects of enhancing normal living conditions; and by the requirement for 'income maintenance' and 'income support'.

According to Indira Hirway (1995), "The concept of social security, therefore, implies a broad pro-poor approach which has three major components; namely a promotional component that aims at improving endowments, exchange entitlements, real incomes and social consumption; a preventive component that seeks to avert deprivation in more specific ways; and a protective component (also known as safety net measures) that is yet more specific in generating relief against deprivation."

The above definitions have been instrumental in the scope of social security were extremely useful in pointing out a different dimension of social security in developing countries.

According to W.A. Robson, "Social security is a way of ensuring freedom from want or poverty which is one of the formidable obstacles in a way of progress. Social security implies insurance against the misfortunes to which an individual remains exposed even the condition of society as a whole improves. It does not include the various measures for improving the conditions of society-full employment, minimum wage, factory laws, public health, education and so forth.

Social security has to be seen, as pointed out by the commentators quoted earlier, in the context of the overall needs of the unorganised sector.

The approach and concept must be an integrated one. However, in practical terms, it is necessary to separate the programmes connected with the provision of these basic necessities. The programmes and activities connected with the provision of employment, income and assets required to reach all basic standard of living may be termed as 'economic security'. Those connected with other basic needs, such as health care, childcare, old age pension, food etc. be termed as social security. Subrahmanya and Jhabvala, (2000)

SOCIAL SECURITY AND LEGAL PROVISIONS: INDIAN PERSPECTIVE

As noted earlier, the unorganised sector is a major contributor to the gross national product of the country, contributing about 63 per cent of the country's national income in 1995. This indicates the urgent need to deal with issues of social security for these workers.

In India, the system of social security was started with the organised sector. The first social security legislation was the Workmen's Compensation Act, 1923, which provided the worker with financial compensation in case of accidents in the course of his work. This was followed by the Employees' State Insurance Act, 1948, which covered medical costs and risks of the workers; the Employees' Provident Fund and Miscellaneous Provisions Act, 1952, which provided for some security after the working life was over. These Acts were followed by the Maternity Benefit Act, 1961, to compensate for loss of earnings during maternity, and the Payment of Gratuity Act, 1971, to compensate for loss of employment.

All these Acts are applicable to certain occupational groups in regular employment in comparatively large establishments such as factories, mines and plantations employing 10 or more persons. In a course of time, while the application of the Acts was extended to more and more such groups, the large mass of workers tended to remain uncovered by any social security.

ILO, for the first time in 1986 recognised the need 'to address, the question of how better to assist in all respects, the masses of the unorganised workers lacking adequate social protection.'

However, it soon became apparent that extending social security to the unorganised sector was not merely a matter of extending existing organised sector schemes to new groups. First, it was found that the unorganised sector is not a homogeneous category. Employment relations vary considerably and are very different from those of the organised sector. They comprise following categories:

(i) Those who are employed on a more or less regular basis, in establishments, which are outside the scope of the existing social security legislation;

(ii) Those who are employed as casual labour, intermittently on contracts, with uncertainly regarding employment and income;

(iii) Those who are own-account workers and producers, including small and marginal farmers, who may occasionally hire the labour of others;

(iv) Those who do a variety of jobs from day to day, from season to season, and often even within the same day;

(v) Those who are seeking work like migrant labour;

(vi) Those who can no longer work.

Second, a major obstacle to introducing contributory social insurance schemes for the unorganised sector is the difficulty in identifying the employer.

Third, unlike the organised sector where steady and regular employment is a given fact, unorganised sector workers need employment security, income security and social security simultaneously.

Fourth, the needs of these workers vary from those of the organised sector. e.g. since a large proportion of the unorganised sector are women, and child oriented needs become increasingly important.

In the Indian context, the concept of social security is derived from the provisions of following Articles of the Constitution:

1. Article 38 of the Constitution, which requires that the State should promote the welfare of the people by securing and protecting – a social order in which justice – social, economic and political – shall inform all institutions of national life;
2. Article 41 requires that within the limits of its economic capacity and development the State should make effective provision for securing the right to work, to education and

to public assistance in case of unemployment, old age, sickness and disablement, and in other cases of undeserved want;

3. Article 42 requires the State should make the provision for securing just and humane conditions of work and maternity relief;

4. Article 47 requires that the State should regard the raising of the level of nutrition and the standard of living of its people.

Economists on ILO's Definition

Various authors have considered that this definition may be too narrow for the problems faced by developing countries. Guhan (1994) claims that social security in poor countries will have to be viewed as part of, and fully integrated with, anti-poverty policies such as employment guarantee and food security. Getubig (1992) defines social security for the developing countries as any kind of collective measures or activities designed to ensure that members of society meet their basic needs (such as adequate nutrition, shelter, health care and clean water supply), as well as being protected from contingencies (such as illness, disability, death, unemployment and old age) to enable them to maintain a standard of living consistent with social norms'.

Economist on Security

Dreze and Sen (1991), as well as Burgess and Stern (1991) distinguish two aspects of social security, which they define as the use of social means to prevent deprivation (promote living standards) and vulnerability to deprivation (protect against falling living standards). The focus of social security is to enhance and protect people's capabilities to be adequately nourished, to be comfortably clothed, to avoid escapable morbidity and preventable mortality. According to them, the concentration on income in the literature on poverty derives from the fact that a shortage of income is one of the most visible and crucial factors restricting the basic capabilities of many people. In addition to the problem of persistent deprivation, there is also the issue of vulnerability. The average experience of poorer populations understates the precarious nature of their existence, since a certain proportion of them undergo severe – and often sudden – dispossession and the threat of such a thing happening is ever present in the lives of many more. The decline may result from changes in personal circumstances (such as illness or death of earning members of the family), or from fluctuations in the social surroundings (such as a crop failure, a general recession, or a civil war).

SOCIAL SECURITY IN DEVELOPING COUNTRIES

In the literature on development issues, it has often been assumed (explicitly or by implication) that developing countries are too poor to be able to 'afford' social-security systems. There are good reasons, however, to question this assumption. It is true that the complex and expensive programmes of social insurance and income maintenance that now form the backbone of social security systems in the richer countries would be difficult to replicate in poorer countries. But there is no reason why these particular schemes should be seen to represent a universally relevant model of social-security provision. Public involvement in direct support to be vulnerable sections of the population (going beyond simple reliance on economic growth and market mechanisms) can take a wide variety of forms, and many of them have already been used with considerable success in some of the poorest countries of the world, (Dreze and Sen, 1991).

HISTORY OF SOCIAL SECURITY IN INDIA

Historically, the system of social security of India, as elsewhere, was started with the organised sector. The first social security legislation was the Workmen's Compensation Act, 1923, which provided the worker with financial compensation in case of an accident in the course of his work. This was followed by the Employees' State Insurance Act, 1948, which covered medical costs and risks of the workers; the Employees' Provident Fund and Miscellaneous Provisions Act, 1952, which provided for some security after the working life was over. These Acts were followed by the Maternity Benefit Act, 1961, to compensate for loss of earnings during maternity, and Payment of Gratuity Act, 1971, to compensate for loss of employment. All these Acts are applicable to certain occupational groups in regular employment in comparatively large establishment such as factories, mines and plantations employing 10 or more persons.

LEGAL PROVISIONS OF SOCIAL SECURITY

In the Indian context, the concept of social security is derived from the provisions of Article 38 of the Constitution, which requires that the State should promote the welfare of the people by securing and protecting a social order in which justice—social, economic and political—shall inform all institutions of national life. Article 41 requires that within the limits of its economic capacity and development the State make effective provision for securing the right to work, to education and to public assistance in case of unemployment, old age, sickness and disablement, and in other case of undeserved want. Article 42 requires that the State should make provision for securing just and humane conditions of work and maternity relief. Article 47 requires that the State should regard the raising of the level of nutrition and the standard of living of its people, and improvement of public health, as among its primary duties.

These provisions are in accordance with Thomas Paine's Rights of man which states that society owes subsistence to citizens either by procuring work or by ensuring the means of existence to those who are unable to work. The Right to Work enables a person to earn his livelihood through work. If for any reason the person is not able to work, society has to provide him with the means of livelihood by other means. Society has, therefore, the obligation to provide everyone either work or other means of livelihood. The two rights are complementary to each other.

REVIEW OF LITURATURE

Unorganised Sector and Social Security: Sociological Interpretation

In recent years there has been a growing awareness of the existence, importance of the needs of the unorganized sector.

The unorganised sector according to Subrahmanya R.K.A. and Jhabwala R. (2000) refers to no clear-cut employer-employee relationships and lacks most form of social protection. On the other hand, organised sector workers are distinguished by relatively regular salaries, jobs with well-defined terms and conditions of employment, clear-cut rights and obligations and fairly comprehensive social security protection.

The unorganised sector workers and producers include agriculture labourers, small and marginal farmers, forest workers, fisher folk, bidi rollers, garment stichers, construction workers, rag-pickers – people involved in an innumerable variety of tasks and employment. Having no fixed employer, these workers are casual, migrant, home-based, own-account workers who earn a living from whatever meagre assets and skills they possess.

Since the concept of unorganised sector that deals with communities or individuals that do not have permanent and secured income, jobs and means of production as well the required professional livelihood skills. The subject has hence been studied in detail mostly by economists such Kannan K.P. (2004), Dreze and Sen A. (1991), Subrahmanya and Jhabvala (2000), Guhan S.

Sociologist did make reference about this phenomenon by using the terms such as 'class struggle' by Karl Marx, 'Division of labour' by Emile Durkheim, 'authority and power' by Max Weber. 'Social struggle' and 'social mobility' by Sorokin. All the above-mentioned sociological views are from some or the other way are talking about the struggle and progress made by individuals of class in the European societies.

Contrary to class system in the West, India is a typical example of caste system, which is the backbone of social hierarchy and stratification. Like Karl Marx who talks about haves and have nots about classes in West, Indian class system too depicts haves and haves not meaning the upper castes groups having command and possession of natural and human resources, while the lower caste groups with meagre resources have been struggling for survival. Numbers of Sociologists, both from India as well as abroad have written about the hierarchy, purity and pollution concepts, social structure and relationships within caste system etc. However, not many sociologists have researched and documented the struggle and insecurities of livelihood faced by the lower caste groups who have been deprived of natural resources, opportunities of progress, rights of protection and development as well in various unorganised sectors.

Jan Breman, a German Sociologist who has researched extensively among the unorganised sector communities of Gujarat since 1960, till recently he came out with a book captioned, 'Footloose Labour—Working in India's Informal Economy' published in the year 1996. In this book he has cited examples of non-agrarian communities, stone quarry workers, sugar-cane workers, diamond cutters, road construction and building construction workers, brick-kiln workers etc. While expressing his views on the unorganised sector, Breman Jan, (1996:3), suggested that, the informal sector also called the unorganised sector, is a part of urban economy; secondly, it lacks clarity concerning its size and dynamics and finally the assumption that self-employment is a principal mode of employment. Breman has used the term 'Informal Sector' for unorganized sector. He further points out (1996:6) that the informal sector is meant to function as a waiting room for unskilled rural workers who manage to migrate to urban destination. After a period of adjustment and skillful formation this first generation of workers then somehow find their way upwards to the formal sector.

In this research it was observed that the younger generation of stone quarry workers, and more precisely among the Lamans who are progressive community, take up skillful jobs such as driving trucks, tractors, bulldosers and operating crushing machines, tar boilers etc. Furthermore, the research has proved Jan Breman's assumption that progress in the younger generation especially among the Lamans, who have taken up jobs such as supervisors, contractors as well as transporters.

Jan Breman's Views on Stone Quarry Workers

In the years 1972, 1982, 1984 and 1986 when Breman visited approximately 10 quarries in the sub districts of Chikhali, Valsad and Pardi in South Gujarat he made following sociological observations:

- **Exploitation**

The private owners exploited all the workers and labourers of the ten quarries.

- **Work-gap in Rainy Season**

Due to open-caste mining and stone breaking, quarry work would stop in rainy season by giving the break to workers till October.

- **Method of Extracting Stones**

The quarrymen wrenched loose chunks of rock, which they then broke-up with sledge hammers. Their wives carried these smaller lumps to a level stretch of land where they and the children hammered them to pieces.

- **Family as a Working Unit**

Breman, (1996: 75), also reported that men, women and children all work together in family groups. The stone-hewers were men helped by their wives, for whom this work was additional to their agricultural work in the neighbouring villages.

- **Supervision by Contractor's Agent**

In each quarry a contractor's agent keeps an eye on production and administered its progress.

- **Replacement of Locals by Migrant Workers**

The most significant change from the view point of Breman (1996: 76) was complete replacement of local workers by migrant workers, he visited another quarry in Valsad, sited alongside the river, where he found a contractor from Saurashtra who had hired stone hewers from Maharashtra for the season. He had brought them that year because, in his opinion, the local workers were no good. They reported for work very irregularly and stayed away for days or even weeks at a time. He found the migrants satisfactory.

- **Division of Labour**

Breman also observed a system of division of labourers based on the occupations, done by males and females separately. The quarry men wrenched loose chunks of rocks, which were exploded by using dynamites. The men broke these stones with steged-hammers. Their wives carried these smaller lumps to a level stretched of land where they and children hammered them into small pieces. The male stone hewers and their female helpers together with working children were divided into gangs led by a 'thekedar' (supervisor). These gang bosses were responsible for recruitment of quarry workers in the home area as well as for supervising their work.

- **Payment System**

Breman also observed that the quarry workers, especially the women who broke small lumps of stones were paid on per brass basis, i.e. the contents of a field bin equalling a weight of 4 tones. Two such bins filled the trucks in which the crushed stone was taken away.

- **Technological Changes**

Breman also observed that manual labour using cheisels and hammers was being replaced with drillers, use of dynamites and crushing machines.

- **Road Construction Workers**

In 1986, while talking about the road construction workers of Chikhli and Valsad, who were mostly Bhils from Panchmahals, Breman stated that, men did skilled work while women and children acted as their helpers. They ate and slept along the roadside, in a bivouac that was moved as work progress.

Degradation in the Labour Process: Case Studies by Jan Breman

While expressing his views on the quality of labour process Breman (1996: 133 to 135) presented two case studies that of stone quarry and brick kiln workers, wherein indirectly Breman has hinted at the issue of economic and social insecurity. These case studies are as follows:

CASE STUDY NO. 1

Inhuman Work Environment

Breman have seldom seen a more inhuman work environment from the climatological point of view than these saltpans during his fieldwork. Nature does not tolerate any living organism above water other than human workers. On the bare plain, not a single piece of shade can be found against the burning sun and the saltish soil reflects the fierce light on the body. At the end of a day, his eyes were rimmed with red. During the hot summer months the morning temperature rises to such a high level that work has to be stopped at noon for a couple of hours. The work gangs who stamp down the soil of the pans at the start of the season accentuate their work rhythm with songs in which they sarcastically praise the mercy of the bosses who enticed them there, far from home, with their cash advances.

The stone quarries are just as ruthless. The worker who quarry the hills in the middle of the plain do not even have water nearby in which they could once in a while seek cooling during hot summer months, as do the men who work in open mines along the river banks.

'The work is done in the open air without any form of shelter. In the morning hours they work in the shadow of the rock wall, after about 1 p.m. this shadow disappears and work stops until 4 O'clock. Even then, it is exhausting just to say in the quarry without working, with the sun reflecting on the now heated rock face. The men keep fit by regularly taking a dip in the river'. (Koelen 1985: 104).

CASE STUDY NO. 2

Miserable Working Conditions

This case study is about miserable working conditions in brick-kilns. Breman notes that not only adults but also children are victims of the miserable working conditions in the brick works. Their labour power becomes indispensable while they are still quite young, and from the age of six they are wakened during the night to carry the fresh bricks made by their father. While wet, those bricks weigh roughly three kilos. The little children run with one brick each, away from the base plate and into the darkness. When they reach the age of about nine, they are promoted to carrying two bricks. Sometimes their parents wake them up crying from the rags that from their beds. But at night they are the only ones, who sing, trying to give them courage. If they run back quickly they can warm their hands for a few seconds by the wood fire which provides the 'patavala' and 'patavali', the brick-maker and his female mate, with light and warmth in the cold winter nights.

Last night, while the parents were at work, a toddler was badly burned. The little boy, not yet three years old, had scampered to the kiln to seek warmth. There he must have fallen against the hot bricks in his sleep. Wet rags did little to stop the lad's screaming and crying.

'A couple of days later, in another brickworks, I found a girl of about 15 years old who lay on the ground under the couple of jute sacks, shivering with fever. Her younger sister came now and again and shook her gently, trying to get her to go to work, because she was unable to carry all the bricks away from the base plate. The labour power of his sick sister is needed to eliminate the backlog. When that has been done, she can lie down again although for no longer than ten minutes.'

When Breman visited a brick field in Mumbai in 1972, the owner whom he had come to know ten years earlier, took the trouble of going around with him to show that nothing had changed in the meantime. An old woman made use of Breman's presence to ask the 'Sheth' humbly for a favour. Her son had lain in the hut for a couple of days with high fever and could not work. Might he go to the doctor? The implication was that the owner would pay for the consultation and for the medicine. At first he snarled that she had to arrange it through the 'mukadam'. But the mother persisted and followed them around the work site. At last, in view of his (Breman's) company, the patron could do nothing other than to give bad tempered permission. To Breman he said that, there was one sort of medicine that almost always had effect in such cases: stopping the living allowance. 'Then they soon go back to work'.

- **Sexual Harassement**

Owners and supervisors (mukadams) as stated by Breman (1996: 175) repeatedly exercise their authority by demanding sexual services from unmarried and some times married women.

- **Illegally Distilled Alcohol**

Yet another observation made by Jan Breman is that illegally distilled alcohol is drunk in large quantities and quarrels and fights break out about trifles.

- **Women and Hard Work**

Among the cane-cutters it was observed chronic illnesses and deaths are regular due to result of poor hygienic conditions. Each day 10 per cent of the workforce is too ill to work, which does not mean that the others enjoy good health. In the orthodox but authoritative opinion of the 'mukadam', however, fever, diarrhoea, sore throat, sores and other wounds on legs and arms are not adequate reasons to stay away from work. (Breman 1990: 583).

- **Food Intake**

Consumption of food is minimal and consists largely of carbohydrates. Food that includes vitamins, proteins and other elements are too expensive for their budgets.

- **Medical Care**

While studying the brick-kiln workers, Jan Breman stated that, the brick-makers are given prior assurance that, when necessary, the patron will provide medical care and accept the costs of that care. However, from long experience of the contracted labourers know that such promises have no value.

- **Job Insecurity**

A common factor among the heterogeneous mass of migrant workers rotating around this area is the lack of permanent jobs with protective employment conditions such as those that apply in the formal sector of the economy.

- **Physical and Mental Agony**

The disruption of employment has been explained by suggesting that long and irregular hours of work together with bad living conditions create a state of physical and mental agony from which the army of migrants can only recover by retreating every now and then to their place of origin.

SOCIAL INSECURITY: VIEWS BY Dr. ROBIN TRIBHUWAN AND RAGNHILD ANDREASSEN

Dr. Robin D. Tribhuwan and Ragnhild Andreassen in their book captioned *'Streets of Insecurity'*, (2003) have given the concept of insecurity. According to them contrary to the concept of security there also exists a concept of insecurity, as already shown by some of the definitions of security. By human insecurity they mean the inability of an individual, a family or a community to cope up with the standards mentioned of better livelihood. As regards the permanent pavement dwellers their insecurity can be understood better from the diagram given below. Although the situation of the temporary pavement dwellers is more complex and they generally enjoy a higher degree of security, we will also investigate this group along the same lines. In the book 'Streets of Insecurity ' Study of pavement dwellers in India', Dr. Tribhuwan and Andreassen have given following aspects of insecurity:

1. Food insecurity
2. Economic insecurity
3. Physical insecurity
4. Insecurity of civil amenities
5. Communication insecurity
6. Health insecurity
7. Mental insecurity
8. Personal insecurity
9. Socio-cultural insecurity
10. Religious and spiritual insecurity
11. Recreational insecurity
12. Educational insecurity
13. Political insecurity

SALIENT FEATURES OF SOCIAL SECURITY

From the review of literature presented in this chapter, it is evident that the concept of social security is a brainchild of social scientists. The said concept has been studied by Economists, Activists, Social workers, Sociologists and Anthropologists, as it is multi-diamensional. Given below are the salient features of the concept of social security:

(i) The term social refers to a society or community life, or to the idea of solidarity. Thus, security according to Hamainun Juha and Horst Singh (2005) is seen as something intrinsically human, in terms of a need, a value, a human right. It is a multi-dimensional concept dealing with different economic, social and political systems and ideologies and theories. Social security is generated by the society in the sense of solidarity;

(ii) According to ILO, social security means the protection which society provides for its members, through a series of public measures against the economic and social distress that otherwise would be caused by the stoppage or substantial reduction in earnings resulting

from sickness, maternity, employment injury, unemployment, invalidity, old age and death; the provision of medical care, and the provisions of subsidies for families with children;

(iii) Social security represents a guarantee, by the whole community to all its members, of the maintenance of their standard of living or at least of tolerable living conditions by means of redistribution of income based on National Solidarity Subrahmanya, (1994). Here, there is a stress given on the obligation of society to maintain all its members in 'tolerable living conditions';

(iv) Any kind of collective measures or activities designed to ensure that members of society meet their basic needs (such as adequate nutrition, shelter, health care and clean water supply), as well as being protected from contingencies (such as illness, disability, death, unemployment and old age), to enable them to main a standard of living consistent with social norms (Getubig, 1992);

(v) Jean Dreze and Amartya Sen (1982, 2002) distinguish between two aspects of social security— 'protection and promotion'. The former is concerned with the preventing a decline in living standards in general and in the basic conditions of living in particular. The latter has the objective of enhancing normal living conditions and helping people, overcome regular and persistent deprivation;

(vi) The concept of social security, therefore, implies a broad pro-poor approach which has three major components: namely a 'promotional component that aims at improving endowments, exchange entitlements, real incomes and social consumption; a preventive component that seeks to avert deprivation in more specific ways; and a protective component (also known as safety net measures) that is yet more specific in generating relief against deprivation Hirway, (1995).

To sum up social security concept implies, a broad pro-poor approach by the employers, the State, N.G.Os and the people themselves against deprivation of basic needs, facilities, amenities, value and rights.

ANALYSIS

An analysis of the views by social scientists on the concept of social insecurity reveals following salient features:

(i) Social insecurity according to Hamainain Juha and Horst Singh (2005) is the result of insufficient care, which expresses itself in anxiousness and uncertainity. There is good reason for defining social insecurity together with the concept of social problems; hence all the insecurity people experience in their life cannot be placed under the heading of social insecurity, only that which results from social problems. Social insecurity is met with through unemployment, poverty, criminality, lack of social care and other social problems;

(ii) Social insecurity can be measured by asking for people's subjective experiences and by using objective indicators.

There are two different areas of social insecurity in person's everyday life regarding the concept of life management – different social risks, threats and dangers (external living conditions) and coping with them (internal state of affairs). Both factors should be taken into consideration in measuring people's subjective experience of social insecurity.

The other side of social insecurity must be indicated by objective quantities. These include not only the rates of employment, criminality, diseases, and other problems but also variables of social care and protection offered by society;

(iii) In their book captioned '*Streets of Insecurity – Study of Pavement Dwellers in India*' (2003; 14) Dr. Robin

Tribhuwan and Ragnhild Andreasen have mentioned that by human insecurity they mean the inability of an individual, a family or a community to cope up with the standards of better livelihood. They have given following aspects of social insecurity:

1. Food insecurity
2. Economic insecurity
3. Insecurity of civil amenities
4. Communication insecurity
5. Physical insecurity
6. Health insecurity
7. Mental insecurity
8. Personal insecurity
9. Socio-cultural insecurity
10. Religious and spiritual insecurity
11. Recreational insecurity
12. Educational insecurity
13. Political insecurity

(iv) Sociological View

Jan Breman (1996) in his book, captioned 'Footloose Labour' has indirectly talked about the various types of social, economic, health, nutritional, political etc. insecurities faced by the stone quarry workers.

In his own words, he has stated (1996: 264) that this book has been written to throw light on the mechanisms of exclusion from life and work in dignity of poor people in high economic growth. Their plight, subsistence not far above the level of survival is shared by a considerable part of mankind. Breman has given examples of sand, stone quarry, road construction, brick kiln labourers and sugar-cane cutters in his book.

SALIENT FEATURES OF INFORMAL/ UNORGANISED SECTOR

The term unorganised sector is also termed as informal sector by certain social scientists. Given below are salient features of the concept:

(i) In an overview of unorganised labour by Press Information Bureau (18th September 2001) Government of India, classification of unorganised workers and characteristics of unorganised labour have been given, which are as follows:

Classification of Workers

Unorganised workers may be categorised under the following four broad heads, in terms of:

- Occupation
- Nature of employment
- Specially distressed categories; and
- Service categories

Small and marginal farmers, landless agricultural labourers, share-croppers, fishermen, those engaged in animal husbandry, in beedi rolling, beedi labelling and beedi packing, building and other construction workers, leather workers, weavers, artisans, salt workers, workers in brick kiln and stone quarries, workers in saw mills, oil mills etc. may come in the first category.

Attached agricultural labourers come under the second category.

Toddy tappers, scavengers, carriers of head loads, drivers of animal driven vehicles, loaders and unloaders, belong to the especially distressed category. Midwives, domestic workers, fishermen and women, barbers, vegetable and fruit vendor, newspaper vendors etc. come under the service category.

Characteristics of Unorganised Labour

- There is no authentic data on unorganised workers.

- The unorganised sector suffers from cycles of excessive seasonability of employment.
- Majority of the rural workers do not have stable and durable avenues of employment.
- The workplace is scattered and fragmented.
- There is no formal employer-employee relationship between small and marginal farmers, sharecroppers and agricultural labourers.
- In rural areas, society is highly stratified in as much as the sociological factor based on caste and community considerations is based on structure of relationship and functioning in that society. In urban areas while such considerations are much less, it cannot be said that they are altogether absent as bulk of the unorganised workers in urban areas are basically nothing but migrant workers from rural area.
- Agricultural labourers and sharecroppers, who are mostly landless and belong to Scheduled Caste and Scheduled Tribe communities. They are heavily dependent on the landlords and moneylenders for everything.
- Workers in the unorganised sector are usually surrounded by a lot of fads, taboos and outmoded social customs like child marriage, excessive spending on ceremonial festivities etc. which lead to indebtedness and bondage.
- The exploitation of a large section of unorganised workers, particularly, those, belonging to Scheduled Caste and Scheduled Tribe, can be attributed to the existence of malfunctional and dysfunctional middlemen.
- Primitive production technologies and feudal production relations, which are rampant in the unorganised sector, do not permit or encourage the workmen to imbibe and assimilate higher technologies and better production relations.

(ii) The I-UNDP Employment Mission to Kenya (1972) identified the main characteristics of the informal sector which are as follows:

- Ease of entry
- Reliance on indigenous resources
- Family ownership of enterprises
- Small scale operation
- Labour intensive and adapted technology
- Skills acquired outside the formal school system
- Unregulated and competitive markets.

(iii) *Social Security Experts on Unorganized Sector*

- The unorganised sector has no clear-cut employer-employee relationships and lacks most forms of social protection.
- The unorganised sector is not a homogeneous category.
- Women particularly are confined to unorganised sector employment, with 96 per cent of all female workers being in this sector.
- In unorganised sector there is difficulty in identifying the employer.
- In unorganised sector employment relations vary considerably, and are in any case very different from those of the organised sector.

(iv) *Jan Breman's Sociological View*

Jan Breman (1996: 3) uses the term 'informal sector' for the concept 'unorganised sector'. According to him informal sector is past of the urban economy and lacks clarity concerning its dynamics and finally it is based on the assumption that self-employment is the principal mode of employment.

To conclude, the concept of unorganised sector is a part of urban economy, consisting of labourers from Scheduled Castes, Scheduled Tribes, Nomadic groups and other economically and socially backward groups, who suffer from cycles of excessive seasonably and uncertain employment, with no formal employer-employee relationship, and those who are regular customers of social insecurity.

In India studies on unorganised sectors, social insecurity and development issues of the labourers become significant as most of them are migrants, landless nomadic, Scheduled Caste and Tribe category and of course socially, economically, educationally and politically less empowered. This piece of work will certainly contribute in developing not only sociological but inter-disciplinary theoretical issues in social sciences.

PROFILE OF STONE QUARRY WORKERS

A site on the outskirts of cities having hills or mountains that having been partially cut to get stones, with plastic hutments or small houses built by the owners, houses of stone walls with low entrances, clouds of dust and smoke from the crushers, machines etc. always reminds a layman of the stone quarry and crusher communities.

- **Stone Quarry Workers in Maharashtra**

Rapid growth in population demands increased housing and civic amenities. This along with fast growing industrialisation has raised the per capita consumption of building material. Most of the construction material used for civil works has been obtained directly or indirectly from earth's crust. It is evident from the old monumental structures and also from present trend of utilisation of construction material that construction activity and also the nature of architecture depend to a great extent on nature of country's work.

The State of Maharashtra is mostly covered by basaltic rocks and is commonly known as Deccan Trap. Broadly, it is used as building stones crushed and broken stones and sand stone.

According to the Manual on 'State Mineral Policy and Related Matters (Manual)' by Trade, Commerce and Mining Department, Government of Maharashtra, Mumbai (Maharashtra) as on 31st December 2002 the total number of Mining that is 1762 and 250 major mining. In reality the number should be much larger. This means about 88 per cent minerals consists of stone, sand, bricks, murum etc. Of these minor minerals, stone is largest minor mineral in terms of quantity, income to the Government as well as employment opportunities.

Out of total 35 districts in the State of Maharashtra, 11 districts are with intensive stone quarrying and crushing, 18 districts are with medium and 6 are with lower activities. All over mega cities and towns are surrounded with large stone quarry activities.

Minor Mining Stone quarry and crushing sector is categorized as 'small scale' unorganised labour sector. There is contract system and division of labour, 'Tapkar' (Tapkari) and 'Bigari' are two categories from maximum and loading activities.

According to National Sample Survey of 1999-2000, in Maharashtra out of 9.38 crore population, 3 crore 40 lakh are workers, of which 2 crore 75 lakh are surviving in unorganised sector. The 8-year report of 'Santulan' NGO (1997-98), reveals that 70 per cent of the stone quarry workers are from Maharashtra, while the remaining 30 per cent are from other States.

Generally workers in stone quarry/crushing sector belong to socio-economically weaker sections, landless from famine, earthquake affected and tribal areas and survive on 'hand to mouth' earnings.

Approximately 40 to 50 lakh workers all over Maharashtra engaged in stone quarrying and crushing activities and they all are basically landless, migrants of famine, drought, earthquake affected and tribal areas from within and neighbouring states of Maharashtra. According to the information given by Deputy Collector, Mining Department, there are 450 quarries in Pune District.

- **Caste Categories of Stone Quarry Workers**

The socio-economic status of stone quarry workers is extremely marginalised. Over 96 per cent of them belong to lower caste categories classified under Indian Constitution. Nearly 90 to 95 per cent stone quarry workers belong to socio-economically deprived and marginalised communities in

India, they are constitutionally categorised as Vimukta Jati (V.J.), Nomadic Tribes (N.T.), Scheduled Castes (S.C.), Scheduled Tribes (S.T.) and Other Backward Communities (O.B.C.).

- **Living Conditions of Workers**

The prime motive of workers is 'survival'. They live next to stone quarry/crushing sites in the remote areas. The huts are hardly 3 to 4 feet high, covered with temporary iron or plastic sheets and walls made up of loose stones. In general there are absolutely no basic amenities, most pathetic and unsecured.

Workers have neither birth nor death records—no ration cards—not enrolled in voting list—neither included in population survey—no benefits from any Government schemes—no health safeties, schools or social securities.

- **Migration of Workers**

One of the unique phenomenons of stone quarry worker's community is their unregulated, unfierced, uncertain and continuous migration from one stone quarry across the districts and state along with their family. Within 6 months to one year, over 70 per cent families migrate from stone quarry to another, 30 per cent within 2 to 5 years and about 10 per cent are seen who remain for more than 5 years at one place.

- **Children in Stone Quarry**

Work pattern of stone quarrying/crushing is of contract basis. The workers get into mining with the sunrise and return with the sunset. Children are either left to them or taken to mining to assist in work.

Generally, the day of stone quarry children is allotted to:

- House works includes food preparation; fetch water, washing clothes, guarding doorless houses etc. Generally these works are the responsibilities of girl child;
- Taking care of siblings. This is the most common responsibility;

- Reaching food to parents in the mining site mostly by male child;
- Assist parents in mining works. Future of stone quarry worker's children is decided at very childhood age. Practically, all of them are left with no alternative but to join the parents in their works as they grow.

Children of stone quarry workers community are the most vulnerable and victimised under the deprived conditions from their fundamental rights.

RESEARCH QUESTIONS

Based on the review of literature on the concepts of unorganised sector, social insecurity, social struggle in informal sector and pilot study carried out among the stone worker communities following research questions were developed to find solutions to. These research questions are as follows:

(i) Majority of stone quarry workers belonged to those caste and/or nomadic groups, whose traditional occupations were associated with stone work, construction and transportation of building material?

(ii) Lower the level of social, educational, economic, political, development awareness, empowerment and status in an individual, family or community, higher the degree of social insecurity?

(iii) Greater the degree of economic insecurity lesser the chance of financial support and loans from banks and financial institutions.

(iv) Lesser the degree of professional skills and literacy level, higher the degree of exploitation and insecurity in an unorganised sector.

(v) The percentage of hiring migrant and semi-nomadic labourers stone quarry owners, rather than local labourers, is higher in most quarries.

Keeping in view the above theoretical background and research questions, the present study aims to unveil the issues of social insecurity among the stone quarry workers by studying following objectives.

OBJECTIVES OF THE STUDY

(i) To study the socio-economic and ethnographic background of the stone quarry communities;

(ii) To understand the health, nutritional and environment problems and insecurity faced by stone quarry women and their children;

(iii) To explore social security provided by stone quarry owners, Government and non-Government organisations to stone quarry workers, as well the communities themselves;

(iv) To unveil the issues of social insecurity among the stone quarry workers;

(v) To suggest a module of social security for stone quarry workers.

SIGNIFICANCE OF THE STUDY

As mentioned earlier, the term social security is seen as something intrinsically human, in terms of need, value and human right. It is a multi-dimensional phenomenon dealing with different economic, social and political systems, ideologies and theories. Hence, at the theoretical level this study will not only be useful in developing theoretical insights to Sociologists, but to Economists, Anthropologists, Development Experts, Social Security Experts and Political Science researchers as well. The facts and observations reported in the study will certainly be a base for social scientists to develop new theoretical insights and ideologies.

At the more practical level this study will be useful to policy makers and administrators of the Government Departments such as Women and Child Welfare, Tribal Development, Social Injustice and Empowerment etc. so as to evolve social security plans and development programmes for the stone quarry workers. The study will be useful to NGOs and Activists working for stone quarry workers, as well.

2

RESEARCH METHODOLOGY

LOCALE OF THE STUDY

The present study was conducted in two areas/villages namely—Moshi and Yewalewadi in Haveli blocks of Pune District in the State of Maharashtra.

TARGET POPULATION

The target population for the study was household heads who were stone quarry workers working in stone-quarries in Moshi and Yewalewadi villages. The target population belongs to four communities/nomadic groups namely: Wadar, Laman, Beldar and Tirumal. 150 respondents were selected from two villages – 142 from Moshi and 8 from Yewalewadi.

METHOD OF DATA COLLECTION

Primary and secondary—both the sources were used to collect the data for the study:

- ***Primary Data:*** Primary data was collected from 2 villages by designing an interview schedule for the household heads. Besides this, an interview guide was also prepared for medical practitioners to find out health and nutritional problems of stone workers. Observation method and photographs were used to validate the primary data;
- ***Secondary Data:*** Secondary data was collected from the books on castes, nomadic groups, unorganised

sector, social security and social insecurity, labour problems, articles published in journals and newspapers etc.

RESEARCH TOOLS

An Interview schedule was designed to gather information relevant to the topic, from the respondents. A pilot study was conducted in order to develop questions in the schedule. 150 interview schedules were administered. Besides this, interview guides were used to find out health and nutritional problems among stone quarry workers. Case studies of some patients, observation method and photographs were also used to validate the data.

In order to understand health and nutritional problems of the stone quarry workers an interview schedule for medical practioners was designed. Four medical practitioners practicing near Moshi and Yewalewadi stone quarries were interviewed. Prof. Vandana Kakrani from PSM Department B.J. Medical College was consulted to guide the researchers to analyse data on the nutritional status of children below 5. Based on primary data their Body-mass Index was plotted and nutritional grades of children were plotted using international standard tables.

Table 2.1 reveals village-wise number of schedules administered, to gather data from the stone quarry workers.

Table 2.1

Village-wise number of schedules administered

Sr. No.	*District*	*Block*	*Villages*	*No. of Schedules*
1.	Pune	Haveli	Yewalewadi	8
		Moshi	Moshi	142
		2	**2**	**150**

SAMPLING PROCEDURES

The sample was selected purposively. The Stone-workers do not stay in their house on holidays. While on working days for 10 to 12 hours working on crushers and stone quarries.

Thus use of random sampling method was not possible hence the researcher chose to go for purposive sampling. Efforts were made to keep in view representative sample from a camp of given community.

ANALYSIS

Qualitative and quantitative both the methods were employed to analyse the data. Statistical indicators were entered in excel software to analyse quantitative data. Simple tables on various indicators such as caste, age, sex, marital status, education, family size, annual income, occupation, borrowing behaviour, type of house etc. were tabulated. Qualitative data was analysed manually. Both quantitative data and qualitative data contributed in analysis and interpretation of facts gathered. Simple tables plotted through quantitative data were interpreted and presented in appropriate places and contexts in the M.Phil thesis. Qualitative data from primary and secondary sources was presented in the form of case studies so as to answer the questions why the stone-workers have set of given problems of social insecurity and analyse why they behave the way they do.

CHAPTER SCHEME

Data gathered, analysed and interpreted through this study, has been presented in seven chapters namely.

Sr. No.	*Chapter*	*Title*
1.	One	Introduction
2.	Two	Research Methodology
3.	Three	Brief Ethnographic Profile of the Lamans, Wadars, Beldars and Tirumals.
4.	Four	Socio-economic background of Stone Quarry Workers.
5.	Five	Health, Nutritional and Environmental issues of stone quarry workers.
6.	Six	Social Insecurity among stone quarry workers
7.	Seven	Summary, conclusions and recommendations

3

BRIEF ETHNOGRAPHIC PROFILE OF THE LAMANS, WADARS, BELDARS AND TIRUMALS

ETHNOGRAPHIC PROFILE OF THE LAMANS

(i) Population

According to Dr.Ambedkar Research and Training Institute, Pune (1991) the estimated population of Lamans in Maharashta is 9.54 lakhs.

(ii) Geographical Distribution

Lamans, also called Banjaras, who were originally living in the northern India were a nomadic tribe who travelled throughout the length and breadth of our country and settled down in various parts of our country. The name differs according to their places of settlement. Lamans are found all over India barring a few small north-eastern States of Sikkim, Meghalay, Arunachal Pradesh, Nagaland, Mizoram, Manipur and Tripura (Dr. Naik D.B.)

(iii) Origin

Mythological, Historical and Social Background: (Naik D. B. 'Lambanis of Karnataka)

There is no exact idea about the origin of each culture. Therefore one has to depend upon the mythological and historical legendry stories. Against this background one has to find out the origin of culture. The legends are not exceptional regarding their origin. There are number of mythological and historical points contained in their legends. Efforts are being made to find out the origin concerning these points.

(i) Mythological and Historical Evidences

Evidence 1

Once God sowed the seeds in the sky. Out of which a maiden produced a child, which was born out of the perspiration of that maiden. She felt sex urge, which was refused by the boy. Afterwards another boy was born who also refused her. The third boy consented to her request. The first man created out of their sex enjoyment, later a number of children were born, and out of them, Karna, was the son of Kodhwaj. His son was Kashappa. Kashappa had two sons – Tida and Cheda. Cheda's sons were city people. Tida had sons named Natadad, Jogadad, Khimad, Mota and Mola. His son Natadad became a pioneer of Wagri progeny who depended on hunting. The descendents of Jogadad became Jogis. The decendents of Khimadad are blacksmiths. If the descendents of Mota became Marovadi-Labana, Mola's descendents became Lamanis.

Evidence 2

The Lamanis are the descendents of Wali and Sugreeva. Out of five sons of Tida, Mola was a divotee of Krishna. He was well versed in dance and music. When Krishna left Radha in Gokula, Mola became servant of Radha. These two, who were experts in dance and music, began to exhibit their dance in the kings' palaces. The King of Dhanaji enjoyed their performance of Art and told them that they would be gifted what they liked most. Since they had no male child they demanded only one son of the king. The King gave his son to them. Later on he becomes the descendent of the Rathod sect. This couple Radha and Mola exhibited their performance of dance and music in the darbar of Bhanogad. They got his son as present; this son became the descendent of the Pawar sect. The son of Jangatgad King later on became the originator of the Chavan sect.

Mola was enjoying his life with three sons. When they became grown ups, he was more concerned about their marriage. Once during herding of his cows near the riverside, he met a Bramhin and consulted about his sons' marriages. The Brahmin expressed sadly his helplessness in marrying off his three daughters. Mola proposed that his three sons could marry three daughters of the Brahmin. Mola, a man belonging to Krishna caste, performed marriages of three daughters of Brahmin with his sons. This progeny is Rathod, Pawar and Chavan.

Evidence 3

Cosmic nature is existed out of five elements, which are *agad* (sky), *Jagad* (earth), *Vagad* (air), *dhaj* (fire) and *Koladhaj* (water). The process of creation of universe as follows:

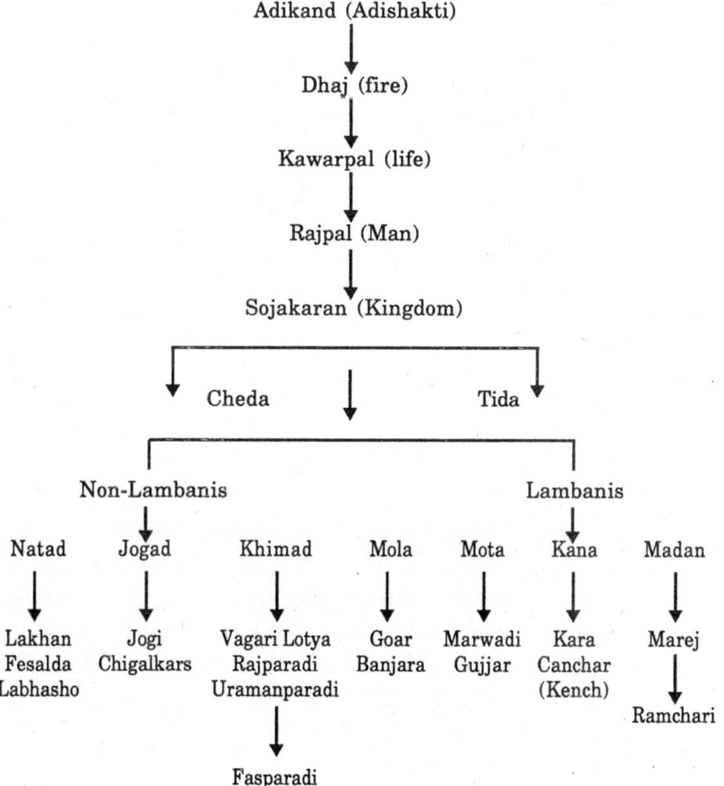

Evidence 4

There were number of royal dynasties ruling in the mountain areas of Arawali. Lakhansingh, the son of Khairagad Rathod of Marwad; Lohansingh the son of Munjin Pawar of Dhara State and Randheersingh Chavan of the son of Toorigad Chavan accompanied Cawarpal, the King of Delhi, during hunting. They found beautiful maidens during the hunting expediations. Therefore they began to tease and tantalise the maidens. Cawarpal, the King of Delhi punished them to stay in the forest. The three princes were ready to undergo the punishment in the forest along with Bhavprasad. They came to a village Khodapalli, during their search of food. Then they moved towards Rakobhan mountain area. Where they were introduced to Nath Labhan, they began to live under his protection. He arranged the three princess' marriage with three daughters of Naga Brahmin. Later on the progeny of Lakhansingh became Rathod; Lohasingh as Pawar, and Randheersingh's progency became to be called as Chavan.

Evidence 5

During the rule of Moghal Kings, minor kings were ruling the small States. The originator of Rajput Dynasty, Rana Pratapsingh was one of them. The Rajasthan State and some parts of Delhi were under his rule. During the time of Moghal rule, King Akbar invaded Rana Pratapsingh's Fort Udaypur. As Rana Pratapsingh felt weakened to fight against the huge army of Akbar; he disappeared into the mountain area, called Haldighat. Number of patriots followed him. Akbar's army began to invade that area.

Rana Pratapsingh was defeated by Akabar's army at Haldighat. Akbar sent a message to Rana Pratapsingh that if he surrenders himself to Akbar, then he would return his land to him. Patriot Rana Pratapsingh did not accept his proposal. He took an oath that he would get back his land only on the battlefield. A number of families migrated along with him into the forest. Akbar started various ways to harassing Rana Pratapsingh; the Rajput families, who accompanied Rana

Pratapsingh, followed the oath of their King and had to face a number of hardships. Finally Akbar defeated Rana Pratapsingh.

The Rajput communities like Marwadi and Gujjar could not tolerate the harassment meted out to them by Akbar. So they returned to their land. Some families remained at the forest and began to lead the nomadic life. Later on these people began to be called as Lambanis.

There are number of legends available about the origin of Lamanis. There are differences of opinion about their origin as they are found in the legends. Some of them say that the Lambanis are originated from the Aryans; and some of them take their origins to the Drawidians origin. The majority of these legends trace that Lamanis belong to the origin of Aryans. The scholars who have studied the origin of Lamanis have accepted this view, some differences of the opinion still exists.

(ii) Written Evidence

In the ancient days the main profession of the Aryans was trade. During this period people known as Pani were doing the business of transaction, and were very popular. Therefore they became the enemies of Aryans. They began to be called as 'Pani'. They were engaged in business. By making study of culture and heritage of Pani people, it is found that Lamanis are one of the branches of Pani Communities. Animal husbandry was a common profession between these two communities. The women were covering their heads with cloth known as *Kangu*; even today this practice is continued. Similarity between Pani community and Banjara Community is found the basic point of the profession and the cultural traits. Banjara people give the names like 'Pani', 'Bani' and 'Dani' to their daughters. The Aryans invaded the 'Pani' community and looted their property and wealth. Knowing this, the Lamani people became nomadic, who were engaged in business and trade. Afterwards these people were called as Banjara, Lamani, Lambhani, Brajwasi and Labhani.

Divergent opinions are found about the origins of Lamanis among the scholars. As for the majority of scholars, "The

Lamanis were originally from 'Rajasthan' and who were engaged in business. They were carrying the goods on the cattle" (Co. Mackenzie, 1881:152; Thurstan E. N. 1909:214; Nanjudayya and Anthiyyer, 1928:136; Chidanandmurthy, 1970:09; Shersingh Sher, 1883:73; Fisher, 1990:61). But Tod Saheb, the historian, who studied the history of Rajsthan states – "There was one community which was carrying on business and trading by carrying articles on backs of camels. Many points of similarity between the community of Banjara and Bhumia are observed. Therefore the people belong to Bhumi caste, later on began to called themselves as Banjara."

Many scholars opine that they are called Lamanis because they were transacting the business of selling salt. There is a reference regarding this community in "Dashakumar Charita" (6th Century A.D) by the famous Sanskrit writer Dandi.

There are different opinions among the historian scholars about the origin of Lamanis. The States of Sindh and Baluchisthan which have become the parts of Pakistan were once the land of Lamanis. These people resisted the foreign invaders of India in the past. The people have bravely faced the invasion of Alexander, the Great and the Moghal King. They converted themselves to tradesman and were engaged in supplying foodgrains to many parts of the northern India.

During the 17th Century the Marathas became prominent rulers in the South. At that time, the Lamani business was flourishing at the highest point. The Peshwas in Maharashtra were importing sugar, spices and dry fruits from foreign countries. At that time the Konkan coastal harbours namely Nagotan, Mohad, Balsar, Panvel and Kolandi were very busy centers for trade and commerce. The responsibility of transporting these heavy merchandise to the nook and corner of India was resting on the Lamanis. "The goods were unloaded at these ports carried in land to various markets over the long distances by huge caravans of Lamanis who were sometimes numbered as many ten thousands," (Chitnis, K.N.1990: 352).

When their trading was prosperous there was a great change in their business i.e. supplying foodgrains to the warriors at the war field. Later on they served as suppliers of foodgrains to the soldiers to Moghals, Marathas and finally British soldiers. Therefore the supplying business was more profitable than the common business. Probably the soldiers protected them. During the Peshwa's rule in 17th century the two Lamani trading leaders named Pomaji Nayak and Govinda Nayak had made business agreement with the rulers to supply foodgrains being carried on the back of 1500 bullocks. For this reason the octroi tax was waived off (Crock, 1987:150).

It is also observed that they changed the process of trading for their convenience. The scholars have recorded that their business center of trading at North and the Central India was transferred to South India at a very later period. General Brigs has recorded in his book, published in 1813 that "Khankahan, the ruler, ceased and taken to custody a big group of bullocks and sent to Gulbarga city, the capital of South India, in the year 1417. Ferista, the historian calls these people as foodgrain merchants. They were nomadic people engaged in business and were travelling throughout the length and breadth of India." The entry of Lamanis into South India during 1417 is an available record. Here is very much noticeable that they were called as foodgrain merchants.

The Lamanis continued their ancient trade which was not confined to India but was extend upto "South Africa, Afganisthan, Khaibar, Italy (Chamanlal, 1969:146), China, Tibet, Arabsthan and Brahmadesh" (Rathod:6)

The Lamanis played dominant role in the national and international trade and also adventureous task of supplying foodgrains to army.

During the Medieval India, the Lamanis had maintained trade links with Egypt, U.S.A, European Countries and Italian City. The Lambardia was their trading center, some families who had gone on trade to European countries later settled there. They are of these families who have settled in Europe, America and Africa are known as Romanees Gypsies (Rupla Naik, 1988:2). There are many similarities in the Roma Gypsies and the Banjara Lamanies.

Source of Inscriptions

The Moghal Kings were highly appreciative of their honesty, valour and integrity. They appointed Lamanis for supplying of foodgrains to their army camps. Asaf Khan had made an agreement with the Lamani leader named Jungi and Bhangi for supplying of foodgrains to his military camps. That agreement is seaked on copper plate that is:

"Ranjan Ka pani

Chappar Ka ghas

Din ke teen khoon maf

Aur janha Asaf khan ke ghode

Vanha Jangi-Bhangi ke bail Khade."

"O Banjara if you find scarcity of water, you can take water from the big earthen pots, preserved at the house of Nawabs. If you find scarcity of fodder for livestock, you can carry the bundles of thatch, covering the huts. During supplying of foodgrains your act of killing any assaulter is pardoned. Wherever the horses of Asaf Khan are there may be oxen of Jangi-Bhangi".

This sealed order of Asaf Khan shows that, Lamanis were having the major role in the work of supplying foodgrains to the army and also it shows Nawabs love and trusts reposed in the Lamanis.

The down fall of the Moghal Empire caused some people to be benefited and some put to loss. The introduction of railways in our country during 1860-65 had a severe impact on them. The railways badly affected the business and trade of Lamanis. How can there be competition between the railways and the oxen? Gradually, their trade began to dwindle. As a result they were unable to look after their large number of cattle. They had to survive by selling them. The Lamanis became vindictive against the British government for ruining their livelihood. The British government, for some time, considered these people as "criminal tribes". These Lamanis who belong to Arya Kshatriya were scared of the assault of the British government and went to settle in the forest.

(iv) Sub-groups of Laman

According to Dr. D. B. Naik, Sub groups of Lamans are as follows:

1. Goar
2. Mathura or Mathure
3. Dhadi
4. Sanar
5. Navi
6. Dhalia
7. Shingadya
8. Maru
9. Bamania
10. Bagora
11. Digora or Gigora
12. Chavan
13. Badi
14. Bajigar
15. Jogi or Bharava
16. Rohidas
17. Dhan-kute

According to Bhagirathi Chowdhury, there are four Vansas/ Subgroups viz. (1) Chauhan; (2) Panwar or Pambhar; (3) Rathor; (4) Burthia or Urthia.

Each group is subdivided into number of exogamous groups known as 'gotra'.

(v) Clans

There are number of clans found among sub-groups of Lamanis. According to K. S. Singh; (1993), the names of clans are as follows: Rathod, Pomhar, Chavhan, Vadatya, Korra,

Jharbale, Ortia, Banod, Kerut, Mur, Mocha, Bhakia, Lasria, Blhot, Jathot, Barmaot, Badaot, Sangra, Bora, Parhia, Murhaot, Nurhaot, Nayek, Baloch (Dhanot), Mashalu, Khadyal, Bajata, Palyal, Salor, Khatyar, Mangroor, Chaghyal, Chandle, Bhatti, Tarwai, Bhanaor, Bhamoria, Hajoria, Chanbadia, Ghanbadia, Bhardwaj, Juar, Ghanarach, Manhas, Khokhor, Bhatti.

(vi) Dressing Pattern

The Laman or Banjara community is one of the many Indian communities, which are mostly known for their various coloured ornaments, bangles and dresses in the colourful garbs. Lamani people can be identified by their dresses. The dress of Lamani woman consists '*Ghagra* (Skirt), *Kachli* (Choli), *Orhni* (head cover) Sachidananda and Prasad R.R. (1996)

There is some anecdote about this fact since the Lambanis were Kshatrias; they were lovers of war, who participated in number of wars. Once when wife of a brave warrior was preparing her garments, she was told that her brave husband became a marty. By throwing away the unprepared garments, she rushed towards her dead husband. Afterwards the Lambani women thought that the leftover garments were incomplete in shape. Later on they began to wear this fashion of dress, which is incomplete. Therefore even today the same designed garments are in use.

The part of their body, which cannot be covered by skirt and choli, they began to wear head cover. (Dr. D.B. Naik)

The dresses of garments, which are worn by Lamani women are embroidered in different coloured pieces of cloth, are stitched on which small piece of glasses are inlaid. These pieces of glasses on their garments reflect the movement of the wild animals. On the other hand these colourful garments scared these wild animals. The pieces of small glasses on their garments were helpful in getting themselves protected by the attack of the wild animals.

A woman is a votary of beauty. She loves both colourful dress and ornaments. The Lamani women, who are the lovers of the nature, are not exception. They like putting on coloured garments and ornaments. Therefore, from head to toe their body is covered with ornaments. In order to protect some parts of the bare body from the bushes and thorns they put on different ornaments on parts of the body. The Lamani women are living in the midst of vallies and forest. So they can prepare ornaments easily, like ivory and wooden bangles. They also wear metal ornaments. Chains having bells are worn in order to produce sound and music, which can force the wild animals to run away.

The Lamani women decorate almost all parts of the body like nails, chest, neck and feet. These ornaments are heavy and having their own distinct designs and shapes. Edgar Thurston says, "Their dress is peculiar and their ornaments are so signularly chosen that we have, we are confident seen women, who had eight to ten pounds weight in metal or ivory round their arms and legs." (1909:235).

The garments and ornaments have been given utmost importance by the Lamani women. The garments worn by a maid, married woman and widow are quite different. The widowed woman is prohibited to wear the colourful special garments and wifehood ornaments.

A married woman is given liberty to put on any kind of ornaments. A maiden is prohibited to wear golden nose ring (*Bhuriya*), a skirt (*Phetia*) and a head cover (*Chantia*). But she can put on chains with small bells on the ankle.

The Lamani men folk wear the common dresses namely Shirt, Dhoti, Turban, and Pagadi. Now-a-days the use of Pagadi is losing its use. In place of it, the turbans are used. They also wear golden earrings, bracelets and silver chained belt round their groin. (Dr. Naik D.B.)

(vii) Language/Dialect

According to Naik D.B. the Lamanis speak Goar boli, which belongs to the Indo-Aryan family of Languages. It has no scripts and independent history though it does not have scripted, it keeps them culturally and socially united. Wherever they live, they understand their language without any difficulty though their language comprises of many loan words and expressions from other languages.

As per linguistic survey of India (1921) Dr. Grierson records the existence of 179 languages. He writes about the Lamani language, "as for their language in many of the countries, they have lost their dialect and use their local language of the non-Lamani majority population of the areas of their settlement. But in the area of their concentration the Lamanis have successfully retained their language Banjari."

Banjari language has been influenced by Sanskrit, Hindi, Rajasthani, Marathi, and Gujarathi and also by other local languages.

Though many other languages have influenced the Lamani language, still it has retained its own identity. In this language we find many words that are not found in the languages listed in the Indian Constitution.

All Lamanis irrespective of their places of residence speak some words. For example: *Goar* (Lamanis), *Koar* (non-Lamanis), *Chora* (Lamani-boy), *Chori* (Lamani girl), *Tandro* (Lamani man, husband), *Gonni* (wife), *Leriya* (bridegroom's helpmate), *Vansali* (flute), *Geriya* (youngster) etc.

These facts indicate that the Lamani language has independent existence. Other Indo-Aryan languages and even Dravidian languages have influenced it. In spite of this influence it has retained its distinctive character as it belongs to a group of Rajasthani language.

(viii) Traditional Occupation

Originally, these Lamanis are the merchant class of Rajsthan who have become very popular among the trading communities like Gujjar and Marwadis. They left this original place for some reasons, migrated towards South India and spread all over the area and become nomadic tradesman. Since they had good number of livestock, which were used for carrying heavy articles. It is found that some nomadic community took up the trade of selling salt, foodgrains, spices and pearls. A fact is known that during the period of Maratha and Moghal rules they were appointed to supply foodgrains to the army cantonments at different places, (Dr. Naik D. B. 'Lambanis of Karnataka')

(ix) Food Habits

According to Karve (1954), Lamanis are occasionally non-vegetarians. Rice, Jowar, Bajara, Wheat and Ragi are their staple cereals taken with pulses, like tur, moong, beans and urad. Men and women occasionally take alcoholic drinks, which are purchased from market and also brewed at home. Smoking beedi and cigarette, and chewing betel leaf and tobacco, are common habits among them.

According to Singh K. S. Lamans in Orissa are mainly vegetarian but some of them occasionally take non-vegetarian food. Wheat and rice are their staple cereals and mahua seed oil (*dulitel*) is their cooking medium. In Haryana, their staple of food consists of vegetables, pulses and unleavened wheat bread (chapatti). Those who eat eggs are considered vegetarian. Mutton is occasionally consumed by some of them. There is a discernible shift from non-vegetarianism to vegetarianism. Mustard, linseed and vegetable ghee are used as the cooking media. They drink tea, milk, lassi and various other soft drinks. Their men occasionally take alcoholic drink.

According to Dr. Naik D.B., originally the Lamanis are non-vegetarians. The easily available fruits and roots, the flesh of hunted birds and animals are their food. Though they are non-vegetarians, they don't eat all kinds of flesh of animals. But they eat only the flesh of selected animals and aqua creatures. They eat flesh of the rabbit, antelope, goat, sheep and other aqua creatures like fish and lobster are eaten as food. They eat the flesh of birds like pigeon and other birds.

Staple food of region like Jowar, Wheat, Bazra and Ragi are used as food for the Karnataka Lamanis. A proverb is in usage that a person who eats Jowar bread would become strong and stout. This shows that they like Jowar bread very much.

(x) Settlement Pattern

The settlement patterns of the Lamans are popularly known as 'Tandas'. The 'tandas' are of two types, one those settlements that are found on the border of Maharashtra-Karntaka, Maharashtra-Andhra Pradesh, border where the houses are permanent and strong. The members of such tandas are more or less settled and practice agriculture as they have land and livestock. The second type of tanda is characterised by temporary huts, which are encroached on fallow or wasteland either possessed by the Government or by the private owners. Members of the second tandas reflect nomadic and semi-nomadic type of life.

(xi) House Types/Housing Pattern

Lamanis construct cottages, which are made of twigs and dry grass. Such habitation is called '*Jupada*'. A stonewall or a mud wall is built around it, and pillar or neem tree or toddy tree is planted in the center place. Afterwards piece of wood and grass are placed and adjusted. They don't make windows for any room. For the passage of air into the cottage a small door is made. For sending out the smoke coming from the hearth is to go out pole from the corner of a cottage. An area having length of 3-4 feet and breadth 2-3 feet is for the kitchen and the other part is provided for poultry and sheep. In the remaining area of cottage the family members will have to stay.

This is a special arrangement for accommodation and breeding sheep, fowl for livestock. Special manager is constructed in the form of cottage. Next is for the chicken and pen for the sheep is made (Dr. Naik D.B)

(xii) Family Pattern

Here and there joint family system is found among this community. Generally independent family system exists. Since patriarchal system is inforce the right to property, community and titles are continued from father to son. Widow marriage and marrying the wife of deceased brother is special systems. The alimony system is strictly followed. (Dr. Naik D.B.)

(xiii) Marriage Pattern

Family and marriage are the ancient and important institutions of human society. The sociologists opine that a marriage between male and female is to continue progeny and to provide sexual satisfaction to the couple. This marriage institution is a consent given by the society. The role of marriage in society is to control extra-sexual affairs of man and woman by which the wheel of social life move on easily. The rituals and process of marriages are different from one caste to another, and from one sect to another. The rituals among the Lamanis' marriages are entirely different from the rituals prevailing in the Hindu caste. Their marriage consists of their own cultural traits. It is believed in the Lamani society, a marriage is a link, which unites male and female, and two families. Therefore it has very important role in bringing nearness and unity between the two families.

Marriages among same sects are prohibited, but the marriage between 'Bhukiya' and 'Jat' sects are allowed to take place. But these two sects are not allowed any one belonging to their inner groups of sects. Because they considered that these two sects are having brotherly relationship. Due to the strict observation of this rule, discipline is strictly protected. Girl and boy are not allowed to select their own spouse, according to their liking. This is the tradition of Lamanis. The responsibility of selecting bride and bridegroom is of parents. Parent's decision is final in the matter of divorce of the couple.

There are different phases in the Lamani marriages. Mainly engagement (*sagayi*), presenting betel nuts and betel leaves (*Gol opani*) and marriage (*Waya*) are the succeeding steps.

- **Widow Marriage**

Widow marriage is allowed among Lambanis. If a woman's husband is dead during her middle age, then she can marry anyone to her liking. But unmarried man refuses to marry a widow. Therefore marriages are performed only between the couples of widow and widower. It is generally found that a widower can marry unmarried woman by following the marriage rituals. But this freedom is not given to widow. This widow marriage is known as "*Rand biren ghul ghallero*" (Naik D. B.)

- **Marriage of Divorced**

If the divorce is not allowed among the couple when things are beyond control, then both husband and wife will be separated in Lamani community. If the wife is unable to be accepted by her husband, then she could marry any person to her liking. This system is called as '*Dashanin ghallero.*' The person who marries may not be married. If he becomes widower of his wife separated from him, then the marriage in second time she will not allowed to take her children born from first husband. But a man can accept the children of his first wife in to his family. The marriage of widow, widower and divorce are performed in a very simple way. (Naik D. B.)

- **Marriage with Brother's Wife**

This system is prevailing among the Lamanies. After the elder brother's death his widowed wife should not have illegal relationship with other men. Further, she should not suffer as a widow throughout her life, and her children should not be orphaned and the prestige of her family should be maintained. Against such background a younger brother can marry widowed wife of his brother. But marrying the wife of deseased younger brother is not permissible. Such marriages are very few. If the family members of the deseased person agree, then the widowed wife can marry any person she likes. She cannot claim any rights for the property of her deseased husband. She handover her own children to the hair of her dead husband and then she could live in another man's house. (Naik D.B.)

- **Polygamy**

If a woman doesn't conceive a child for a period of three or four years and if she is found barren, then there is scope for second marriage. A person can marry any number of ladies. But this liberty is not given to woman; so far as a family progeny is concerned they are very rigid. If a woman remained issueless then her status will be disgraced in the society.

The Lamanis are divided into patrilineal exogamous clans. These clans regulate marital alliances and indicate social status and descent. There has been a change in their surname, i.e. Lamani has a changed to Naik. Marriage with one's father's sisters, mother's brother's or elder sister's daughter is allowed. Levirate and sororate (junior) are permitted. Adult marriages are practiced, which are settled by negotiation. Monogamy is the norm. Marriage symbols (of women) are upper arm rings (*Chuder balya*), pendants (*ghogri*) and thali. Dowry is paid both in cash and kind. Neolocal and patriocal rules of residence are followed. Divorce is allowed with social and judicial approval on grounds of adultery, maladjustment, etc. Divorce compensation is given to the wife's parents. Both men and women are allowed to divorce and the children continue to live with their father. Widow, widower and divorcee re-marriages are allowed. (Singh K. S, 1993)

(xiv) Religious Rituals

(A) Birth Rite

The Lamanis strictly observed external purity during ceremony of birth and death.

The Lambanis strictly observed external purity during ceremony of birth and death. When a woman's delivery is fast approaching, a special accommodation for her is prepared. Generally the accommodation place for her delivery is cattle manager because a house, according to Lambanis, means only a big room or a tent. Therefore there was necessity for making special arrangement for a pregnant woman. It is also observed that during the delivery period the family deities will be felt as impure. For this reason a special accommodation is made. Water that is being used for providing a bath to the delivered mother is not allowed to flowout. But it is made flow into a ditch in the manager. This is a blind belief that, if anyone crosses over the water, then the mother's milk in the breast will be dried up; and also it is believed that the evil spirits go on torturing both mother and the child.

The delivery work is being performed by an experienced woman at the house itself. Even today also this custom is followed. Elderly woman are experts in the delivery work. The bunches of nerves at navel are cut off and are hidden under the earth in a pit near the house. This is covered with *'gerukayi'*, a coin and palmful of flour. It is placed in a very safe place. It is believed that if a dog or crow or other animals eat these articles then both mother and child will have to face sufferings and breast milk is dried up. When the cut part of the navel is dried up, it will be tied into a piece of red cloths and tied around the neck of the child. Because it is believed that the child will be prevented from being attacked by the evil forces. This belief is generally found in the Lamabanis of Karnataka.

- **Vekal Peeyer**

It is a religious ritual, which is performed on the occasion of birth of a male child. The elders will consult the foretellers about the birth time and name to be given are discussed with him. Afterwards the mother will be provided a drink, a glass of decoction made out of coconut, Jaggery, Ghee and black pepper. Afterwards the child is given bath. Incense smoke is prepared in order to appease the deities. The experienced elderly women will stand in a line in front of the house and offer prayer songs to the family deities, which are called as "*volang*". After performing these rituals of worship a sweet dish called *'khand'* prepared out of mixing coconut, Jaggery and flour is presented to the childless married women.

During this joyful celebration, the father of the child will provide liberally liquors to the elders of the *'Tada'*. This indicates that much prominence is given to the birth of a male child in the Lambani society. But this kind of celebration of joy and gaiety is not found on the occasion of the birth of a female child.

- **Dalawa Dhokayero (Jalawa Dhokayero)**

It is a religious ritual, which is performed to give an end to the period of impurity for the mother and child. This ritual is carried out on the seventh day of the delivery. *Jalawa Dhokayero* means offering salutation to the water. Touching and worshiping water mitigate the impurity.

A small pit is dug up infront of the house, where a woman has delivered a child; the area around the pit is plastered with dung. Four lamps made of dung and flour is litup, at the flour directions of the house. A flame is prepared in the pit with small sticks. The elderly women will present rice to the mother and new clothes to the child. Five young boys place seven pots painted with lime and black colour decorated on the head of a mother. Carrying the pots, the mother will be marching slowly towards the pit, slowly throwing the grains of rice on the ground. Then the boys will bring down the pot from the mother's head. The mother has to touch the dung-plastered part of the area with her thumb of the right leg for seven times. Then she has to go round of the pit with flames. Then the mother will wash the feet of the five boys and salute them. At this time the elderly women of the *Tanda* will offer a prayer song to the *Chatimata*.

After completion of the ritual and prayer, water is poured into the pit. Then the boys will place the pot on the head of mother. Again mother has to go round the pit. She will enter the house by throwing ricegrains on the ground. The assembled children will be distributed a sweet dish, called "*Kullar*". It is known as a sacred food. This item is an ending point of the delivery period. Then afterwards mother is allowed to touch some articles in the house. These rituals are even today observed in the Tandas of Karnataka by making some changes here and there. Mother will have to spend one month's time along with child at this accomodational place. Then she will return to original place.

The naming ceremony of the child is very simple among the Lambanis. The names of a child, which is pre-consulted, will be uttered into the ear of a child in a cradle. The invited elderly persons and children are presented a sacred dish call '*guggari*'. Here ends the folk rituals.

(B) Tonsuration Ceremony

The cutting of the first hair of the newborn child is a religious ritual among all the castes of Hinduism. It is observed as a special festival in Karnataka. The tribal Lambanis celebrate this festival in ritualistic way. The boys are forbidden to shave their hair without performing the tonsure ceremony. There is no distinction between the male and the female child in respect of tonsure ceremony. The Lambanis have some fears about performing this ceremony. They feel that untonsured children will become tempernmental, physically weak and disaster will be in the family affairs. Therefore due to these fears the Lambanis have given greater importance for the observance of this ritual.

On the tonsure day they clean their whole house. A small crescent shaped bower is setup in the centre of the house and installs their family deity. A sheep is offered as a prey, for each child who is meant for tonsure. Afterwards the children are made to sit in a line before the deity. The Lamani barber or the father will cut off the child's hair in Law's (mothers brother) of the child. The person who has tonsured child's hair will be presented with rice, cloth and some amount of money as present. In the evening sacred '*prasad*' food is made of flesh of sheep, which is offered to deity. After offering prayer to deities all the elders of the family distribute this sacred food as a '*prasad*' to all the assembled people. People belonging to same sect are awakened throughout the night and beat bronze plates drum and cymbals and sing songs of ballad in praise of deity. In the early morning once again they perform prayer—'*arati*'- and distribute the *prasad*. With these items this important festival comes to an end.

The Lambanis collect the child's hair, which are tonsured and put them into a small cloth bundle and make it in to float in the flowing river. The Lambanis are superstitious that if a dog urinates on this hair of a child, then its head will have ulcers. There is another fear that if a child's enemies, they would take revenge and destroy the family by taking the help of black magic and sorcery. Therefore the Lambanis take utmost care in making it safe from the hands of the enemies.

(C) Menstruation

The state of Puberty is a natural condition for both male and female. For a matured girl of Lamanis, there is no other special observation. A matured girl considered as woman. This girl is made to stay outside the house for a week, under the supervision and observation of an elderly woman. Everyday she is fed with very nutricious food like coconut, jaggery, wheat rava etc., and a Kade decoction prepared out of coconut, jaggery, black pepper and ghee. On the seventh day she is given bath, her bedding dresses are taken in to the house. With this, first measturation period comes to end.

(D) Marriage

Marriage is known as '*Waya*', '*Veeya*', '*Saditanero*' '*Tambu tanero*' in the Lamani language. Marriage process commences from the groom's house and ends at the bride's house. There are three phases of marriage processes methodically. They are '*Wadayi*', '*Mandodo*' and '*Ghota gholero*'.

- **Wadayi Ceremony**

A seal known as '*wadayi*' is stamped on the right shoulder of the bridegroom before the marriage ceremony. It also indicates his entry in to their society. The Upanayana ceremony of upper caste is equal to this '*Wadayi*' procedure of Lambanis. The designs of Rangoli are put at the centre of the house and well-folded gunny bag is placed on the design. The bridegroom and his brothers are made to sit on this bag. In front of them an oil lamp is lit, on the two sides of their seats seven balls of '*Maldi*' (a dish mixed with pices of chapatti and Jaggery) are placed. At the same time porridge (as wheat dish) made out of hand-pounded seeds of wheat and ghee in the flames of hearth fouvered and incense is burnt. Afterwards the elderly women stand in a line and sing a song in praise of Goddess, which is known as "Volang".

The priest of the *tanda* will offer the '*maldi laddus*' to the groom and his brothers. Then a red-hot needle is stamped on the right shoulder of the groom and his brothers. At that time he utters a '*guru mantra*' in to the ears of groom and his brother.

The Lambani community believed that those whose *Wadayi ceremony* is not performed their bodies are liable to be buried.

The Lambanis also strongly believe that a dead person will get Salvation, if his body is burnt. Therefore this "*Wadayi*" process has been given importance. Here, we find two prominent points. The first is procedure of purifying the soul of a person, who has come out through number of wombs in the past. Secondly the purified person should get married and should shoulder the responsibility of the married life. This is the blessing. In some parts of the Karanataka a sheep is offered as a prey during the '*wadayi*' ceremony. In some parts people offer sweet dishes.

- **Putting 'Tilak' on the Forehead**

This ceremony is observed at the time of sunrise. A plate is placed in front of the bride, which contains items like a blouse piece and betel leaf covered with turmeric paste, bracelets of groom and an amount of fifteen rupees. This amount is meant for the nose ring of the bride. This is known as "*nak mandero rapiya*". The brother of bride will put '*tilak*', made out of turmeric paste on the forehead of his sister. She will embrace her brother and go on crying and sings a sad song, named "*Dhavalo*".

Putting a '*tilak*' on her forehead is a significant step that she is passing from maidenhood to wifehood. She is entering in to a new phase of life. The bride who is enjoying imaginary joys is immersed in the sad ocean of sorrow. This kind of expression of sorrow in the sad context is not found amongst any communities in the world. This is one of the distinct cultural traditions of the Lambanis. The bride sings this type of songs knows as '*Dhavalo*' during the programme of pasting mehendi, wears bangles, dressed and putting turmeric paste; these songs are in one style, but dealing with different themes.

- **Saptapadi**

Bride is forced to touch the hand of groom; and is made to go seven times around the '*homkunda*' or a fireplace. During this '*parikrama*' elderly women of the *tanda* sing *saptapadi* song. The Lambanis put wooden threshing rod in the centre in place of *homkund*. The spirit behind placing rod is that their life should be firmed. During the celebration of *saptapadi*, the women folk of the tanda sing a song.

This song indicates the cementing link of affection between the bride and community of the *tanda*. This also shows sentimental and delicate feelings of the bride, which has touched the inner core of the tanda.

- **Haveli**

After the *saptapadi* programme the marriage ritual ends. The groom is made to stay in the bride's house for some days; and he is given to eat nutritious food like coconut, ghee, jaggery and wheat rawa. Afterwards he is bidden farewell along with the bride to his house. The bidding farewell programme is known as "*Hawali Karayer*".

Before this programme the elderly women coach the bride to learn the singing of sad songs under the moonlit night. She is also taught how to sing sad song when she meets her own relatives. This song is known as "*Malero*". They also teach her how to sing a farewell song at the time of departure from her *tanda* to the groom's house. This farewell song expresses her good wishes for the community of the *tanda*. This song is known as '*Haveli*'. A Lambani woman has only one chance of singing of the '*Haveli*' song in her lifetime. There is no scope for '*haveli*' song in other types of union of a couple. The bride will stand backward on the Ox, presented by her family finally, towards the *tanda*. She rises of her hand and sings '*Haveli*' song.

(E) Death Rituals

Birth and death are the two faces of single coin. A person who is born must die. There are certain rituals, which are performed at the birth; similarly some rituals are performed at the time of death. In every caste and community certain rituals are carried on after the death of a person. The Lambanis have got distinctive ways of carrying out of rituals. Even performing the last rites are also having distinctive practice.

Burial and burning of the dead body are prevailing systems among the Lambanis. The dead unmarried and children are "buried" others are burnt in a fire. Generally, people with albino disease are also burnt. In case of that person is not burnt then it is believed that there will be drought in that year.

When the husband dies the '*Mangalsutra*' is snatched away from the neck of wife. The anklets, which are the symbols of wifewood, are removed and the ornaments of hair and '*Khavya*' a part on the shoulder part of the blouse are also removed.

During the funeral ceremony, the son has to carry a pot and move infront of the bier on the middle of the road the direction of the dead body is changed; and one rupee coin is thrown over the dead body. The grain of ragi and *navani* are sprinkled on the road during the funeral procession. People will examine the omens on road. If a fox, a rabbit and snake move from right to left side, they believe that the dead soul will posses the incarnation of those creatures. The eldest son of the dead father will put burning flame on the head side of the body. The pot is broken and thrown on the dead body. The son will beat his father's head with a green branch of tree. This is known as '*tincho dero*'. This act is considered that provides salvation to the dead soul; and the soul will enter the heaven. If the dead person is issueless of male children, then his nearest relatives perform this ritual.

During the return journey from the graveyard, they move towards the tank or stream and touch water. They walk around the berry tree and cut off its leaves and throw them on the ground. The people visit the house of the dead person and express consolation and sympathy for bereaved, and then they go to their houses.

Going round berry tree and placing the dead body facing the ground, sprinkling the grains of ragi and navani signifying that the evil spirit should not come back. The dead body, which is facing ground, will not standup, even if stood up he has go round the thorny tree which requires whole night.

After the death of a person, the third day is observed as, also the last rite. This is known as '*Dadokarero*' or '*Kandya kareo*'. If the person die on Saturday or Sunday this ritual is performed on the same day, because it is believed that these two days are in auspicious. The last rites are not performed on other following days. If a person dies on these two days, it is believed that he is a sinner, wicked and he will become a devil's spirit.

On the same day or second day another ritual is performed. It is known as "*had bhandero*". The chief of the *tanda* will prepare non-vegetarian food of sheep flesh and console the bereaved family members by offering food and liquor. There after the chief will have their food along with other relatives.

The twelfth and thirteenth day after the death of a person is observed as the last rite. This is known as "*Barotero Karero*". The twelveth day's celebration is performed in the house itself and prepares food in the name of dead person and offers the food. If the death day is observed on thirteenth day, it is performed outside the house. They prepare simple hearth with three stones and prepare food. After offering food to the dead person the other near relatives have to eat food. The small flags placed on the ashes identify the birth of the dead person. If the pot is empty, then it is believed that the dead person will became a devil. If it is full, it means that he has entered the heaven.

In this way the rituals performed from birth to death have their own distinctive characteristics of Lambani culture.

(F) Religious Worshipping

The worshiping deities of Lamanis of Karnataka are *Sevabhaya* and *Jagadamba* (*Mariyamma*). Originally Lamanis were *Shakti* worshipers. Therefore, they worship deities of energy like Goddess *Kankali, Mariyamma, Durgadevi, Vagzai, Ingalmata, Chamadmata* and other names. They have strong belief that Jagadamba was the originator of the *Shakti* devata.

The Lamanis worship their cultural hero *Sevabhaya* as the chief and protector of this society. In every *tanda* there are dual temples, defying *Sevabhaya* and *Jagadamba*. The temple of *Sevabhaya* is called as "*Dhuni*". The Lamanis consider the village called '*Pouragad*' in the district of Akola of Maharashtra state, as a holy place of Hindu's like Kashi or Banaras. Because it was the place where their cultural hero *Sevabhaya* breathed his least.

Worshipping of *Shakti* Goddesses, offering of prey and fire worship are usually practices of worship among the Lambanis of Karnataka.

- **System of Offering Prey**

Offering prey is one of the systems of worship among the Lambanis. They offer as a prey, the different animals like sheep, chicken and goats to the *Shakti* devatas like *Jagadamba, Vagzai,* and *Kankali* etc. Different sects worship different goddess as family Goddess; but Goddess *Jagadamba* is worshiped in general. The process of system of worship is one and the same.

- **Kondpuja (Fire Worship)**

The Lambani call this puja '*Bhog lagadero*'. The deities like *Sevabhaya, Chambandmata* and *Satsattis* don't accept animal prey. Sweet dishes prepared in ghee are offered to them, like the worship of the ancestors during the Deepawali festival.

This *Kondpuja* and Lambanis appear similar to the Vedic '*Yadnyas*'. In the ancient days the Aryans were performing the '*Yadnyas*' as a means of fulfilling their aspirations and desires. The Lambanis also continued the same system of worship known as Kondpuja for peace and prosper of the families.

- **Family Deities**

The Gods and Goddesses, which are worshiped by the Lambanis, can be identified as family deities and *tanda* (village) deities. The process of these two worships is similar. The family deities are worshiped during the birth rites and tonsuring ceremonies of the children. If the family facing any misfortunes or disastrous they worship them by offering the prey of sheep, chicken and goats. If there is no special occasion, they offer prey to the family deities after visiting the holy places. Among the chief deities worshiped by them are *Tulajabhavani, Gujaral bhavani, Jagadamba, Vagzai, Kankali* and *Ingalmata*. The family deities are called as "*Gharer Bhavani*" the deity like *Chamadmata* is not offered animal prey.

- **Worshipping of Shakti Goddesses**

Generally the Lambanis are worshippers of *Shakti* devata. They worship goddess like *Satsatti* and *Satbhavani* along with *Jagadamba, Mariyamma, Kariyamma, Durgamma, Chamundi,*

Kankali, Vagzai and *Huligemma*. The *seven-satti* goddesses are sisters and they married great personalities. During the worship of goddess, *Hunasatti, Kesirani, Sitasatti, Bhimasatti, Tuljasatti*, no prey is offered. The Lambani women sing songs hours together confining these goddesses. They express awe-inspiring of these goddess through their songs and stories.

The Lamanis worship the *Satsattis* and also *Sat Bhavani* goddess. They recognise this goddess and respected as *Adishakti*. They plant small stones in their field at the boundaries of their villages. These seven stones signify the seven goddesses.

Tulaja Bhavani, Sital Bhavani, Bhojra Bhavani, Massor Bhavani, Matral Bhavani, Wagzai and *Hingalamata* are the seven sisters, who are worshipped as Shakti devatas. They offer prey to these goddesses. They believe that if these goddesses are not satisfied then the people become victims to the anger of these goddesses. The sickness of children, spreading of diseases, physical aliments of cattle or any havoc is due to these goddesses. In order to avoid the danger and havocs, prayers are offered to these goddesses for their appeasement.

The Lamanis are too innocent and sentimental about the subject of gods and goddesses. Therefore they worship these *Shakti devatas* regularly. They also believe that plague; chicken pox and eye diseases are thought to be as the curse of these goddesses. With a view to prevent such diseases they satisfy these goddesses by offering chicken, sheep and silver eye etc.

- **Sati Worship (Worship of Widow)**

Since the Lambanis are the followers of Rajasthani tradition and conventions they worship *Sati Aradhan* or the worship of a widow, who voluntarily died for her dead husband, who became a martyr. There are different types of worship-*Hunasatti, Sita Satti, Jamani satti, Bheema satti, Rupa satti, Kesirani* and *Gujasatti*. The worship of these seven *Sattis* or widows is still found in their society. Very extension folk literature is available about *satti* worship in the folk literature of Lambanis. This *sati* worshipping system is also found in Rajasthan.

- **Worshipping of Ancestors**

Worshipping of the elders and ancestors is the most important religious system among the Lamanis. Honouring the chief of the family, distinguished people of the society, brave and martyrs is a distinguishing feature of their worship. These worships are conducted during the Deepawali and Dasshera festivals. If they were not worshipped properly then they would be badly affected. They worship the elders during the Deepawali and Dasshera festivals. The worship of elders during the Deepawali and Dasshara festival is known as *'Ghar Gharer Puja'* means house worship. A pray is offered to the elders and also they offer non-vegetarian food and liquor.

During the Deepawali festivals they perform *'homa'* for the elders and offer sweet dishes with ample Ghee. The chief of the *tanda* or the family leader will utter the names of the elders and offer dishes and prayers.

The Lambanis believe that the diseases are caused due to the curse of gods, evil spirits and sorcery, and also discontentment of ancestors. They also believe that diseases are the warnings to the people that they have forgotten the worship of the goddesses. If there is an outbreak of diseases they consult saintly people and obtain foretellers. They also demand preventive methods. They once again remember the forgotton promise to God and surrender to them and try to mitigate the evil effects of the disease by the offering.

- **Black Magic and Sorcery**

Since long man has been trying to master the nature. The nature consists unknown miraculous powers, which are used by man for his benefit. The black magic has sprungout of this belief. The black magic is an art that is not based on scientific methods, but man has aspired to posses the natural powers. This is called as black magic or black science.

The Lambanis are having strong belief as well as fears about the black magic. Their constant wandering in the hilly regions, sufferings due to diseases, illiteracy and poverty force them to believe the black magic. They strongly believe that by practising this black magic they can escape from the assault of the enemies and to take revenge against the enemies.

They maintain some caution to keep themselves away from the black magic. The fallen hair during the combing should not scattered here and there. They are bundled together, packed and kept in safe place. They hide the peeled off pieces of nails in a pit. They believe that if the soil taken from the footprints on the road can be misused for killing the people. Therefore they are careful in stepping.

Among the Lamanis there are two kinds of magic practices. One is protective and the other one is destructive. The protective magic practice is used for individual and social welfare. But the destructive magic practice is used for ruining others.

The main person who practices, this protective magic is the priest, known as '*Bhagat*' and also as '*Bhop*'. He is a professional priest at the temples. If any one is suffering from diseases, this priest will burn the incense in the temple and invite the divine spirit to enter in his body. He would ask reason from the elements and advice him about the preventive measures be followed. If the family Gods and Goddesses trouble the people then he would advise them to express terms of their wish fulfillment. If the devil and devil spirits were haunting the family then he would give various preventive methods. He would ask to wave round the patient the items like half boiled rice, lime, a living chicken and sheep. These preventive methods are against the background of protective magic.

During the contagious diseases also, the *Bhop* or priest will instruct the Lambani people to follow the preventive measures.

The women folk among the Lamanis practice the destructive black magic such women, who practices this magic are called '*Dakan*'. The Lamanis believe that this woman magician will control the evil spirits and make them for their own benefits. These evil spirits are called "*Munjya*". Lamanis believe that the "*Munjya*" evil spirits cause the mass death of cattle, the death of healthy people and to decrease the quantity of foodgrains during the harvest time.

The Lamanis get help from the black magic woman in destroying their enemies. These magicians perform the magic process with the blood of a chicken or a pig or the cloth, used by a woman having monthly menstruation. They also use nails, cut off hair and soil under the feet. The articles used for black magic are hidden under the threshold of the house.

- **Evil Eye**

If any attractive articles appear to be producing bad effect by the glance of the eyes of a person is called as "an evil eyed person". There is a common belief among all communities, that if hale and healthy children, a field enriched with greenery and crops, milking livestocks are seen by evil eyed people, then it will bring disasters. The Lamanis of Karnataka are not exception to this superstition.

Para-psychologists have agree, this fact. After making thorough research they state that the glance of evil eye will bring bad effects. The Lambanis are scared much about the bad effects of evil eye. So many ritualistic practices are practiced for preventing these evil effects.

They believe that a child who is always crying is considered that it was due to the evil eye effect. The Lambanis will move broomstick for seven times around the child's body and it is thrown away. They take pinch of salt and dry mirchy in the left palm of the hand move around seven times and throw these articles into the burning earth; and twist all the fingers of the two hand thereby producing sound. Sometimes they put water and little bit lime in the bronze plate and move around seven times on the body of the child and throw that water on the meeting point of three roads or they take up the soil under the feet of the child and move around seven times and pour that soil on the meeting point of three roads. They feel that these practices will mitigate the evil effects of the evil eyes.

If a child or an elderly person feels indigestion of food it was due to effects of evil eye. A mugful of water moved around the body seven times and it is put tupsytury on the frying pan. If the pot stuck-up firmly to the pan, they they would consider that this is due to the effects of an evil eye. That mug is kept for sometime afterwards it will be removed. Think that all bad effects of the bad eye are removed. If a milking cow does not give milk or if it kicks the milkman then, lime, duly energised by mantras tied around the neck of the cow. Sometimes they also tie sea-shells, small wodden bells, seeds, a piece of antelope's horn are tied in a thread and put round the cow. They believe that this necklace of articles will prevent the evil effects of evil eye.

The Lambanis practice different ways and means in preventing the evil effects of evil eye. Even during this scientific age also there is number of superstitions prevailing among the people of tribal Lambanis. This is due to lack of educational facilities.

(xv) Festivals

The religious festivals help to continue religious faith, meditations and cultural development. The Lamanis, who are nomadic, have been adopting themselves to Hindu traditions and at the same time they have been observing their own religious festivals in distinctive ways. Folk life is pre-dominantly influenced by religious faith. These Lamanis have been worshipping various deities for various reasons. Against this background of religious faith, they have created number of religious festivals and celebrating them in their own ways. They have been maintaining their own culture through religious faith and devotion.

The Lamanis of Karnataka are observing prominent Indian religious festivals in their own distinctive ways. Their chief festivals are *Seetalamata* (*Ashad Devta*), *Dashahara*, *Deepavali*, *Holi* and *Teej*. The festival of wheat sprout (*Gowri*) besides these they also observe the Hindu religious festivals like *Nag-Panchami*, *Yugadi* etc.

- **Teej (Festival of Gouri – Wheat Spourt)**

This festival of *Teej* is mainly reserved for Lamani maidens. Annually this festival is observed during *Shravan* (Aug/Sept) and *Yugadi* (Feb/Mar) months.

They have to get the permission of *Nayak* of *tanda* for celebration of this Teej festival. If there is a good harvest and the people are enjoying great peace and plenty then only *Nayak* accords permission. This festival is continuously observed for ten days. This festival is observed specially by unmarried maidens and the maidens who were shortly going to be married. They exhibit great joy in dance and song. The experienced women narrate heroic songs and romantic songs. They also teach different positions and postures of dancing.

After obtaining the permission from the *Nayak* of *tanda*, the maidens will go to the anthill with caring bamboo baskets. On the way they found the berry tree and then go round seven times the tree. They collect anthill soil in their bamboo baskets and carry it along with seeds, of wheat, manure water and move towards the house of *Nayak*. There the experienced women will pour soil, manure, and seeds of wheat and water in their baskets. Nayak and his wife of *Nayak tanda* offer five bamboo baskets to five unmarried maidens and advice them to place them in the temples by maidens and remember they grow these sprouts *Sevabhaya* or Lord Krishana. She consoles them to protect them with vigilance. In this way the wheat seeds are placed in the baskets in the name of family deity and household deity.

The maidens get up early in the morning and take bath in near by tank or wells. They take bath twice a day. The holy water is poured into the bamboo baskets. For nine days during the festival they only eat very soft food. They have to give up the food prepared out of turmeric. For this they really believe that these sprouts will grow having green colour but not yellow colour. If the spouts of a bamboo basket, owned by an unmarried maiden, have rich growth of sprouts, she will be considered as a chaste lady. Therefore the maidens will take care their baskets more than their life. In this way they protect their baskets for nine days. On the ninth day the baskets containing wheat spourts are thrown into water. On this occasion they invite their relatives. In the morning of the final day of this festival, they place these baskets on the altars of their family deities and offer '*Prasad*'. The relatives will also participate in the programme and present gifts to the maidens. These maidens dance and sing joyfully throughout the day. At the evening time they go to the potter's house to prepare the earthen images of *Gangore* (shiva) and *Gangouri* (Parvati). They go to the tank, river, and canal to bring the clay. Even during this procedure also they dance and sing. The youths appear on the way, they tease and tentalise the maidens. They escape from the youth and go to the potter, who prepares the earthen small statues. These two earthen images are dressed in the male and female dresses, representing Shiva and Goddess Parwati.

The final stage of this festival is to throw these pourted baskets into the well. These spourts are once again worshiped at the house of the *Nayak* of the *tanda*. They present gift on behalf of the tanda and nip some spourts from the baskets. This action made the maiden to have overflow of sorrow. They embrace together and express their sad feelings.

The maidens will take up the spourted wheat baskets and distribute and salute each and every relative. Teej is exchanged as a token of affection. The earthen images representing *Gangour* and *Gangouri* along with spourts baskets are taken to nearby tanks or rivers for submerging by the maidens. At that hour also the youths once again tease and tantalise them and interfere their movements. Humour and comic actions are dominating the youths, which are the characteristic of this festival, which is observed in memory of Lord Krishna.

- **Dassehera Festival**

This festival is known as *Nadhabba* in Karnataka, which is also called Vijaya Dashami and Dasshera.

Generally the Lambanis observe this festival in grand way by offering prayer and worship to their deities like *Sevabhaya*, *Jagadama*, *Durgamma*, *Mitubhaukiya*. Though these deities are generally observed but particular deities are worshiped in the particular areas. If their family and other deities are commonly observed but they offer worship and prayer to appease the deities and special prayer is also observed.

The *tanda* people will meet at *Sevabhaya* temple and take permission and collect all the materials required for the festival. They collect subscription money and food grains from the public. Therefore it is a public function.

For a period of ten days during the *Navaratri* and *Vijayadashami* they worship *Durgamma* and *Sarswati*. On the final day all the community people will assemble at the temple and offer their presents. They perform the mass slaughter of sheep, in front of the temple with a view that their wishes to be fulfilled and all the misfortunes of the future times will to be avoided. This is the heartful prayer to the Goddess. In this way they worship all the family deities including *Mariyamma*, *Sevabhaya*, *Mitubhukiya* with all sincerity and respect. Afterwards mass feeding is arranged for the inmates of the *tandas*. Throughout night they are awakened and are engaged themselves in singing prayers, hymns, narrating stories and mythological story in the name of Goddess.

There is so much of similarity in the festivals of north Indian states like Rajasthan, Gujarat, Madhya Pradesh, and Uttar Pradesh between the Lambanis of Karnataka. Even among the Rajputs there are festivals like *Kaliteej*, *Goparva* (worship of cow) as done in Karnataka.

- **Deepavali**

Deepavali is the occasion of eradication darkness by illumination of lights. This is the most important festival for Hindus. *Dhanalaxmi* (Goddess of wealth) and *Dhanya Laxmi* (goddess of corn) are worshipped with splendor during this festival.

The Lambanis call this festival *Devali* or *Kalimas*. The word '*Kalimas*' means the Goddess Laxmi in the night of Deepavali. The young Lambani maiden, dressed in colourful dresses with lighted oil lamps in their hands, go to the house of the Chief of the Tanda. They obtain the permission for the rite of '*mera*' (*Arati*). They address the song to all the groups on their way to the houses, expressing broadmindedness in wishing good luck to all. They go round the *tanda* at night to instill the spirit of unity and integrity among the Lamanis.

The rite of performing '*Arati*' in every household is known as '*mera karero*'. They offer the *Arati* or light in the name of family gods and the members of the family. They even offer light to the animals and to all the people of the *tanda*. Men-folk give them presents in cash according to their capacity. This '*mera*' tradition resembles the *Antike-Pantike* of Malenadu area of Karnataka and *Ani-pini* tradition in the plain of Karnataka. All these traditions originate from the same source but they are observed in different regions according to their own methods.

On the morning of '*Balipadya*' day (next day of Laxmi-Pooja) the Lambani young ladies dress in colourful garments and assemble with bamboo baskets and go to fields and gardens for collecting flowers. Collecting newly bloomed buds of the new corn and different flowers they return with in the sunrise to the *tanda*. They offer these flowers with devotion to saint Sri *Sevabhaya* and *Jagadamba*. At that time they sing the songs. Making little lumps of dung, collected from the sheds of each house, they offer flowers to them. This is performed in all the houses of *tanda*.

The worship of cow dung is symbolic of the worship of sacred cow, which has a prominent place among their cattle, and deserves foremost worship. They worship cattle with love and devotion. They consider them as their wealth. The cow dung worship of the Lambanis of Karnataka is known as '*Gobardhan pooja*' (cow worship) we find this rite also among the other parts of the Lambanis and also Marwadi people of Rajasthan.

On the same day the Lambanis also offer worship to their ancestors. The important person of the *tanda* or the chief of the *tanda* (*Nayak*) goes in a group and they offer worship to their ancestors in every home. On this occasion they pray to the Goddess of Divali (Deepavali) *Meethubhukiya* and *Sevabhaya* to protect cows with broken horns, ears, mixed coloured cows, rows of oxen and horses in the forest area. They also pray for the wealth and prosperity of *tanda*.

- **Seetala Mata Pooja**

During *Ashadh* month (July/August) the Lambanis perform the worship of Goddess of *Sat Bavani* and *Lukkad* (servant). The arrival of *Ashadh* month brings different kinds of diseases. Therefore, they pray the Goddess of energy like *Tulaja Bhavani*, *Seetala Bhavani*, *Bhojari Bhavani*, *Matharal Bhavani*, *Masoor Bhavani*, *Vagzai*, *Ingalamata* and *Lukkad* (servant of seven Goddesses) to protect them from any kind of diseases and distress.

They take seven plain stones and paste with *suramanj* (red soil) on the face and establish them as the statues of the seven Goddesses and before them one stone will be put as a *Lukkad* (servant) and they pray with sweet dish and with a dish made by meat of goat.

(xvi) Folk Tradition/Culture

In India we find different caste groups, ethnic groups, tribal and nomadic groups. Each group has their own culture and traditions.

(A) Dance

The art of dance has background of religious worship as it has an ancient history. Dance is a means of expressing inexpressible feeling of man through physical actions in a rhythmic way. There is fine harmony between the feelings and rhythmic physical movements. It occupies an important place in the domain of arts. The tribal people have their own distinct tradition of dance. There is no scope for facial expressions in Lamani dance. Their feelings and sentiments are expressed through the physical gestures of the torso, the legs and the hands. The chief feeling in the dance is calmness. The dance is generally performed in every tanda but it has been attached more importance during marriage celebrations and religious festivals. The types of dance may be classified as:

1. Women's dance;
2. Men's dance.

➢ Women's Dance

The Lamani women become one with their dance and songs on many occasions. The songs and dances are performed during religious festivals and marriage ceremonies at *tanda.*

They perform dance with purpose of appeasing 'Sri Krishna'. It is known as *'Teej dance'*. During these occasions the Lambani women perform the dance and sing profusely:

Chori goriye dudiya talav gadalocha

Chori goriye rangi rangiri voma machalicha

Chori goriye pani bharaje vanoon rakaricha

Chori goriye Tandero nayak katagocha

Chori goriye vore bana malav sunocha.

The beginning of each line expresses intense feeling of zeal. They step and dance according to the variation of the music and song. These dances and songs are presented during the festivals concerning 'Sri Krishna' and also other functions. These religious songs and dances are not presented commonly in the functions. These songs flow with sentiments of romanticism. This dance is called *'Kundali dance'*.

➢ The Kolat (Dance with Striking of Small Wooden Sticks)

A dance with rhythmic striking sounds of short wooden sticks, which is known as 'Kolat'. Generally this dance is found in almost all clans of the Lamanis. The characteristic of this dance is singing a prayer song along with rhythmic stepping. A group of 10-12 Lamani women stand in a circle with small wooden sticks measuring about 1-2 feet in their hands and dance in tune with the drum sounds.

➢ Kikli Dance (Dance in Circle)

The Lamani woman performs dance according to the rhythm of the song, without the help of musical instruments, it is known as *Kikli* dance. The women stand very close enough to each other and clap each other's hands and bend their bodies backward and forward and dance in a circle. Sometimes they dance without songs. The characteristics of this dance are the movements of the body. The rhymes are not adjustable to this dance. This dance has a speciality of expressing intense joy and zeal with a rhyming couplet at the end.

➤ Men's Dance

Dance performed during Holi Festival.

The Lamani men dance and sing romantic songs like their women during the celebration of the Holi festival. The men stand in circle and sing a chorus song with movements of the limbs and step according to the rhythm of a song which is known as '*Lengi song*' sung only during Holi festival and prohibited on other occasions. Some lines of one of the *Lengi* songs is given below:

'Ralak talavadi haribhari gundali

Chori Janaki kekada charangeye khet,

Patalima bati hatema dandiya,

Chori Janaki Khageye Khet'

The speciality of this dance is sweet voice and rhythmic stepping, finely blended together. This dance resembles the '*khatak*' of the Punjabis.

➤ Dandia (Dandar Ramati)

The Lamani men perform *Kolat* during the Holi festival. The sticks are about one or two feet long, and they are struck together during the dance. They stand in two opposite rows. Some of them sit and stand and strike the sticks and dance in accordance with drum beating. This dance is called as '*Danda ramero*' (dance with sticks). It resembles '*Zoomri*' dance of the Panjabis and also a popular dance of Baluchistan. The characteristic of this folk dance is that its rhythm, which is generally found to be same throughout our country.

➤ Lezim Dance

The Lamani men-folk perform a dance with lezims (i.e. the wooden sticks tied with chain of small bells), it is called

Lezim dance. The Lezims are decorated with coloured papers and dancers wear colourful uniform. This beautiful entertaining dance is observed during the festivals and fairs.

The characteristic elements of the Lamani dance are as follows: the dance of Lamani women resemebles the Manipuri dance and Kathakali dance of Kerala. The characteristics of Kathakali dance are rhythmic movements of body in background of beautiful songs and gorgeous dress. These are found in Lamani dance. The *'Lengi'* dance and *'Danda ramero'* dance resembles the Punjabi dance, which indicates that the Lamanis are originally from North. There is a close relationship between the Sikhs and the Lamanis.

(B) The Art of Embroidery

The designs of flowers and leaves that are knit by different coloured threads and needles are known as embroidery art. This art is very attractive especially on the coloured cloth. There are designs like tree, creeper, flower, animals and birds. The scope of this art is very vast.

Of all the folk arts of the Lambanis, the art of embroidery is the most important one. It is not an exaggeration if it is said that women do not put on dress and garments without embroidery. They tailor their garments for daily use with different coloured pieces of cloth in different designs of embroidery art. These garments of the Lambanis are really artistic. Stiffness accompanies this art in making the garments. The round pieces of mirror are inlaid on the multi-coloured cloth, which covers them full. The garments are embroidered also with buttons, coins, small bells, etc. There has been a great demand for these garments as fashionable dress in the film world as well as in foreign countries. It is bounden duty of the Lambani society and the government to preserve this art, which is slowly fading away due to the influence of modernism.

The Lambanis call this embroidery art as *'Khilan'* and 'toon'. The traditional garments contain different coloured pieces of cloth and also various designs of embroidery. They call the different types of embroidery with different names.

(C) The Art of Tattooing

The art of tattooing is preserved as the distinct art of tribal folk, having its own religious background. This art has a unique place especially among the folk arts. Having tattoo marks before the marriage ceremony is customary among these people. This art has aesthetic as well as religious aspect. Both men and women aspire to have the tattoo marks engraved on their body.

A foreign tourist by name Tavernier who visited India said, "the banjara (Lambani) have tattoo markings right from the forearms to the shoulder. Different colours were prepared out of many roots and painted the tattoo marks with the colours. The skin appeared as a flower-bed" (Maheswarayya, 1981:468).

The Lambani tribals believe that tattoo marking sanctifies and beautifies the body. They believe that they will not be allowed to go to heaven without tattoo marks. Tattoo marks are put on the particular parts of the body. Some marks are visible and also hidden. This is the specialty of the art of tattooing. After studying different designs of tattoo marks Mr. Thurston said: "This tattoo mark is a decorative art and does not indicate the caste mark".

(D) Folk Musical Instruments

The Lambanis use musical instruments like drum, bronze plates, and cymbal during singing of ballads and narrative poems. Especially the bronze plate is the most important musical instrument among the Lambanis. Owing to the modern influence the other modern musical instruments like tabla, zammaraca, khanjra, they play upon these instruments and sing songs. In some areas they play upon the harmoniums.

(E) The Folk Dramas of Lamanis

There is no dearth of folk dramas in Lamanis. After observing the drama and the folk drama in regional languages the Lamani artists intended to fillup the gap of the folk drama. Therefore, they took up the task of composing the folk drama. They composed some folk dramas like *Sri Sitalpati Maharaj*, *Sri Satya Sevalal Leelamrut*, *Sri Satya Neelavatar* and

Samakimata, etc. These folk dramas were enacted on the stage on the occasions of marriage and festivals. The amateur writers have preserved the cultural heritage of their glorious past. They are responsible for preservation and development of their folk literature.

(F) Lamani Folk Literature

The Lamani community, which is having their own distinct culture and tradition, are quite sentimental in giving expression to their innermost emotions and experiences. They entertain with their songs and dances; which influence, hills, valleys and pastures, smile with a joy. There is fine blend of beauty of lie experience and romantic spirit in each and every song.

They sing songs, pertaining to the different kinds of stages of life like birth, death and sacred festivals. They sing profusely during the marriage ceremonies. As the Lamani women are gifted poetesses. They compose songs on the spot and sing melodiously depicting the sentimental scenes and feelings. They add graceful dance to the songs. Their songs find an exposure to their feelings of joy. They sing song melodiously during the occasions of grinding the flour, threshing, rocking the cradle, cutting the trees and embroidery work and other items of their daily activities. Their songs speak their delicate heart and impart solution and comfort to the hearer.

The types of their to folk literature like songs, proverbs, puzzles have been still preserved. They get relief to their physical pains through singing the meaningful songs, proverbs, folktales and sayings.

➢ Mythologies

There are two main kinds of mythologies amongst Lambanis. Namely, the mythology about the origin of their community and profession are quite distinct. Mythologies are available about the origin of universe, its status and doomsday. They adopt the Indian epics like the Ramayan the Mahabharat and other stories to their cultural context.

The mythologies are mainly about their family deities like *Mariyamma. Sat Satties, Sevabhaya, Hatirambava, Mitubhukiya, Nanusad, Linga Masand, Surasad, Lokamasand* etc. These are long epical poems. There are two epics about their cultural hero like *Sevabhaya* and a saint Hatirambava. The Mythology of *sevabhaya*, having the impact of *Saiva* tradition and mythology of Hatirambava, is based on Vaishav tradition. These two epics are having regional importance.

The lives of Sevabhaya of Pouragad and Hatiram of Tirumale are abounding in innumerable anecdotes. These two longer mythologies throw much light upon the Lambani's life and culture. These two mythologies add more information in their caste systems, conventions, traditions; faiths, practices, marriage life styles, judiciary system; family set up, socio-economic set up, celebration of festivals, deities, rules and regulation and taboos. These two important epics deal about their oral traditions.

➢ Anecdotes

Though anecdotes are imaginary, but contain some truth events and the people can't reject faiths outright. The anecdotes are concerning about mythology of a life of great man, important place and events. Anecdotes are also found in their traditions. They consider anecdotes are not imaginary but as facts. These anecdotes are regional. Such anecdotes are mainly about the Lambani cultural heroes like Sevabhaya and Hatirambavaji. Proofs are even today available about these anecdotes.

It is narrated that Sevabhaya during his childhood was engaged in herding the cattle. He prepared Seera and Puri on the sandy place without fire. The rocks become drums and palm leaves become the cymbals during his prayers.

The Britishers brought railways, whose harsh sound was intolerable to Sevabhaya and changed the direction and position of the railway lines. He gave his symbols and deity symbol; the two flags are white and the other red. He ordered that if the two symbols were not followed then he wouldn't allow them install railway lines.

He was given persons name as Hatiram, because, the Lord of elephant blessed him. He lived on leaves of a tree. One day he was accused by the priest Bavaji stole that diamond necklace of goddess. It was proved that God himself had left that diamond necklace in his hermitage.

Number of anecdotes regarding the birth and death of saint Sevabhaya and Hatiram Bavaji are still popular. These anecdotes have historical importance, truth. The spiritual power of Sevabhaya and Bavaji are having anecdotes among the Lambanis. In short the anecdotes occupy an important place in this community.

➢ Folktales

Folk-tale form is very important in Lambani folk literature. The Lambanis call folktales *Saki* and the stories to be listened as *Samaler Saki*. There is less interest attached to the folktales. The professional singers do not attach much importance to them.

There is no religious theme in the folktales of the Lambanis. These folktales have didactic and entertainment purposes. In these tales the imagination is soaring high. The Lambani professional and amateur singers are reluctant towards them. The folk tales of the Lambanis are narrated during the leisure time while travelling or collecting fuel. The grand mothers narrate the tales on the moonlit night and make the children sleep. The main purpose is to entertain the audience. Nowadays people have least interest in telling or listening the folktales because of the appearance of new audio-visual mass media, like T.V. and Radio in the *Tandas* and also the cinema talkies in the near by cities.

Tales of animals, tales of magic, religious tales, romantic tales, tales of stupid ogres. Jokes and anecdotes and formula tales are available in Lambani folk literature. There some distinct folk tales are available like the tale of *Pitalya Paltya*, *Suriya Chandiya* (The Sun and the Moon), which throw the light on the Lambani culture. In Lambani folk tales a special place is given to the cunning fox.

➢ Folksongs

Expensiveness and variety are the chief characteristics of the Lambani songs. Their cultural heritage is solidified in their songs. The salient features of Indian folk literature are found in the folk songs of the Lambanis. They contain the characteristics of great poetry, sentiments and natural language. Through the study of these rich songs one can find out countless ideas about their cultural life. Their popular songs can be classified as hymns, entertainment songs, women folk songs, and men group song.

Different forms of songs are available in the folk literature of Lambanis. They are chiefly about rituals, religious hymns, songs sung during the physical labour, romantic songs, songs with dance and humorous songs, ample songs about children in the form of nursery rhymes. The chief among them are the songs for marriage rituals, birthday festival (*Dhunder Vanjana*), *Teler Kadi*, *Dhavalo* and *Haveli* songs. These are the distinct songs among Lambanis, which are not available in other folk literature.

Dhunder Vanjana: This song is usually a community song, which is sung on the birthday of a male child. During the Holi festival elderly and young people together sing the songs.

➢ Haveli Song

Before sending the bride to the bridegroom's house, the leading women of the *tanda* assemble under moonlit sky to teach the bride different procedures of weeping for one week. She is taught how to weep when her relatives come to her house, and how to express her pangs with tears. This kind of expressing sorrow through the song is not found in any other community. Her song of well wishing of the parents and relatives is known as '*Haveli*' song. This opportunity of '*Haveli*' song is only found among Lambani women. This is not practised in remarriage ceremony.

Chhuta mat Jayes haveli
Marej nayak bapuri haveli
Tarej rajema achoj khadi
Achoj peedi haveli ahinya
Turej rajema achoj void

The labour songs have the lion's share in the folk literature of the Lambanis. They sing these songs during the work of grinding, thrashing corn, removing the weeds in the fields, splitting the wood, drawing the water and grazing cattle. These songs provide solace to their tired minds. There is a perfect harmony between the song and the action. Such songs are generally found among the Lambani women.

Along with these songs there are other songs reference to the great epics like the Ramayana and the Mahabharat and other religious songs.

➢ Ballad

The *ballad* form occupies an important place among the traditional songs of the Lambanis. The Lambanis call this song in their language as *Thalir geed* (song sung with the beating of the bronze plate) *Nangarar geed* (Drum songs), *Mot geed* (long song) *Penar geed* (Ancient song). The professional singers known as *Dhadi*, during the special occasions, sing these songs. The singer sings about the story of their cultural heroes, throughout the night. Ballad songs are sung during the religious festivals and annual festivals. There are ballad songs that are sung from fifteen minutes to the entire nighttime. The community people of *tandas* will feel blessed by listening these religious songs.

➢ Method of Singing

The Lambani singers sing these narrative ballads in their own distinctive ways. The chief singer will commence singing. The other singers will repeat the first and the last lines of the song. They sing these songs with rhythmic beating the bronze plates and other instruments. In order to make the audience to grasp the idea he would give the summary of the story in a prose order. Then he would continue the story.

1. Religious Ballads

There are religious ballads about *Jagdamaba*, *Sura sevak*, *Jampa Bhagat*, *Hamu Bhukiya*, *Hatiram Bava*, *Nanusad*, *Lingamasand*, *Lokamasand* and other saints and seers. Along with these songs, there are other types of songs like the stories of the widows, who burnt themselves in the fire, namely, *Hunasatti, Kesirani, Sita satti, Bhima satti, Tulaja satti* and *Rupa satti*.

2. Mythological Ballad

The Lambanis were highly influenced by the great Indian epics, the Ramayana and the Mahabharata. The songs based on these two epics are available like *Ahalya* song, songs about *Anasuya*, *Bhaktisiriyal*, *Seetapharn* and omnipotent God Hanuman.

3. Historical Ballad

Originally the Lambanis belong to the Rajput sect of Rajasthan. The prominent events that occurred during the political period of Rajaputs and the adventures are still popular in the Lambani folk literature. The chief among them are *Alaudal*, *Raja gabaru*, *Madu bhukiya*, and *Sidi bhukiya* ballads.

Narrative ballads about heroism: These Lambanis are leading the life of struggle and adventures. The chief among such ballads are Veer Haridasala, Asaldhabi, and Buchcha Lavadya etc.

Wonderful narrative ballad songs: These songs are having the background of wonderful imagination. More importance is given here for imagination than the realism. Numbers of such songs are available. The notable are songs like *Mehata-Purna*, *Saliyar Saki* (story of fox) *Dostir geed* (songs of friendship) etc.

➤ Proverbs

Proverbs have a significant place among the genres of the folk literature. The proverbs having valuable meanings are for all times. The Lambanis call proverbs as *Kahavat* or *Kavate*.

Probably this word *Kahavat* means originally the words used. Among the Lambanis, proverbs are noted for their didacticism, imagination, experience, metaphors and rhythm. The proverbs have distinct place in '*Goar Panchayat.*' They were often used in preaching of moral behaviour expressing specific expressions and parodying other behavior.

Among the Lambanis proverbs regarding profession and caste, plants, animals, birds, insects, food, means of instruments, habitation, family, nature, religion, beliefs, entertainment, jewellary, dress, feelings, wealth, time will be available.

1. The hunter alone knows the footprints of a rabbit.
2. Why the mirror is required to study the palm?

➢ Riddles

Riddles have special place among the forms of Lambani Literature. They entertain and please from the young children to the elder people. The Lambanis call these riddles as *thodersaki* (solution of story), *Jeeter sake* (winning story or question and answer story) and *kabad* and *kalame*. These riddles are found in all their activities pertaining to their practice, concept, faith, justice, morals, religion and tradition. These riddles are prominent during the Panchayat session and *Teej* (sprouts of wheat) festivals.

Riddles are available about different limbs of body, cattle, birds, insects, plants; items of cookery and house hold articles.

For example:

1. A mud pot having nine holes (Human body)
2. While plucking the red, bitten by turmeric (red bee)
3. Snake creeps and pigeon hangs in air (rope and pot)

The Lambani riddles are notable for dealing variety in themes in a very musical and rhythmic in tone. Sometimes these riddles are of other languages. (These are in the question form). These riddles are having prime importance in the Panchayat system. They have still retained their cultural spirit in their inmost heart.

(xvii) Lamani Medical System

- **Folk Medical System**

The Lamanis have strong beliefs in the country medical system. They find out their own method of treatment for number of diseases by surrounding quack doctors, spirit of Gods, magic and sorcery and foretellers.

If any minor disease is spread in the family, then they would consult the elderly persons or experienced man in the *tanda*, and they will get relieved of the aliments by taking home medicines. If one is attacked by cold or cough; then a good quality of liquor is drunk and eaten good food and get a sound sleep, then he can be completely cured of the disease. If any one is attacked by migrane then juice of *Keru* seeds is applied in seven lines on the forehead of the patient. If there is eye trouble then limejuice drops are used for eyes. If eyebrows are swollen then the seeds of ripened mirchi (red spice) are filled in the eyes. If a scorpion or snakebites the upper part of the limb is tied with a rope will be filed as a precaution not to allow the poison to enter the body. One should make small wounds on the bitten parts, so that the poison is allowed to sweep. For this the hard grain gram is given for munching; to make the snakes poison flushed out; they take the root of the black rice. After rubbing they get the juice and patient will be made to drink. The poison in the body will be flushed out through vomiting. If a scorpion bites a person, then it is killed and opened its belly and this belly part will be rubbed on the bitten part of the body.

The Lamanis believed that the diseases are caused due to the evil effects of devils. They also believe that the reason for the spread of plague, cholera and chicken pox are due to the anger of the evil spirit like *mari* and *masanis*. The Lambanis appeal the village deities by offering prey to the village deities like *Mariyamma* and *Durgamma* to speed up the recovery of the diseases attacking children and cattle. If the medications appear failure to treat the patient, then they surrender to the divine spirits. They will consult foretellers and ask for relief measures.

Sometimes they get relief of their diseases through the magicians. Such doctors practicing magic are called as '*Bhop*', *Khazi*, and '*Zhadmarewalo*'. The Lamanis believe that the magician doctors possess unique power of treating diseases. If a child behaves mentally upset or if child suffers from cold or cough these magician doctors will energies pinch of ash talisman, a lime fruit or a black thread, which is to be tied on the shoulder or the neck, this process of treatment will give relief the sufferers. These magicians can cure the snake and scorpian bite and attack of evil spirits. These energised articles are being specially prepared on Thursday and Sunday, by wearing these one can get relief from the disease.

On of the characteristics of blind belief prevailing among the Lambani is that, if a woman becomes issueless, then a pregnant sheep will be killed and offered as a prey to the evil spirit, then that barren woman will become a mother.

(xviii) Economic Background

- **Original Profession**

Originally these Lamanis are the merchant class of Rajasthan who have become very popular among the trading communities like Gujjar and Marwadis. They left this original place for some reasons, migrated towards South India and spread all over the area and become nomadic tradesmen. Since they had good number of livestock, which were used for carrying heavy articles. It is found that some nomadic community took up the trade of selling salt, foodgrains, spices and pearls. A fact is known that during the period of Maratha and Moghal rulers they were appointed to supply foodgrains to the army cantonments at different places.

The advent of British rulers in India brought modern facilities like railway, post and telegraph in India. The railway had to transport the commodities, the Lamanis found it difficult to compete with railways. Their condition became worst. They gave up their profession and adapted to the regional professions.

- **Other Occupations**

There are number of references available regarding their countless livestock under their possesses. Their livelihood was depending upon the animals like cow, chicken, goat, sheep and other animals. From animal husbandry they were getting dairy products like milk, ghee and butter. After making use of some part of it for themselves the excess was sold, for maintaining their family.

Some ladies cut the trees in the forest and sell it as fuel. They collect fruits from the forest and sell them in the market. Some of them collect flowers and forest products and sell those products for their livelihood. Some of them are engaged in the construction of house building, road repair and mining works. In this way the Lamani people are engaged in different professions for their livelihood.

The Lamani women especially do the work of embroidery. They use multi coloured threads and stitch their garments with small piece of glasses. Some of them have made embroidery as their livelihood. In one word a needle is a companion of Lamani woman. Some women sit throughout the day in the house and engage themselves in their embroidery work.

The overall economic condition of the Lambani community is very awful. They find it Himalyaan task for daily maintenance of their family. Some times they do illegal transactions like selling their own children for the orphanages. The Lamani women could not get any means of livelihood. Their own children became big burden to their family. They had to sell their own children. This shows that there is a dire poverty and economic degradation crisis among the Lamani families.

In Karnataka, few of the Lamanis own land, but the majority are landless labourers. Their traditional occupations are trading and liquor manufacture. According to 1981 census, 43.76 per cent of them returned as workers including both males and females. Of them 36.41 per cent are returned as cultivators, 49 per cent as agricultural labourers and 4.52 per cent in livestock, forestry etc. Of the rest, 2.78 per cent were engaged in manufacturing, processing etc. and 2 per cent in trade and commerce. The latter refers to their traditional occupation of manufacturing and trading liquor. The remaining 5.54 per cent of the workers were engaged in various other services (Singh K. S., 1993)

In Orissa also, some of them own landholdings and others are landless. The landless earn a part of their subsistence through agricultural labour. Many of them still continue their traditional salt trade. Their women are expert in needlework with which they contribute to their family income. According to the 1981 census, 39.49 per cent of them are workers, comprising 62.34 per cent males and 17.50 per cent females. Of them 39.40 per cent are returned as cultivators, 29.03 per cent as agricultural labourers and 8.52 per cent in manufacturing, processing etc. Of the rest, 17.28 per cent of the workers are engaged in trade and commerce (their traditional occupation of salt business). The remaining 5.77 per cent are engaged in other activities (Singh K. S, 1993)

In Haryana, Lamanis are reported as Banjara. Most of the community members are petty traders in chilcs, carts etc. They also make sirkis. In cities they sell bamboos, strings and round wooden rafters (ballies) and are self-employed as vegetable vendors, owners of small tea-stalls. There are very few who are white-caller jobholders and government servants. Their traditional occupation is to buy calves and colts in thousands, rear them to maturity and resell them for a profit. According to 1981 census, 29.43 per cent of them have been returned as workers. (49.60% males and 5.63% females). Of them 32 per cent reported as engaged in manufacturing, processing etc. indicating their primary involvement in their traditional occupation of making sirkis etc., 12.49 per cent engaged in trade and commerce, i.e. shopkeepers dealing in clilcs and carts, and running small tea-stalls; 32 per cent as agricultural labours; 5 per cent as cultivators, and remaining 18.27 per cent as engaged in other services. (Singh K.S, 1993).

In the state of Himachal Pradesh, Banjara i.e. Lamani are known as *Labana or Lavana*. They are traditionally associated with trading and peddling. Their population in the state, according to 1981 census, 27.09 per cent of the labans ar returned as workers. As evidenced from the census, as many as 63.44 per cent of the workers are returned under the primary sector of the economy i.e. 49.56 per cent cultivators, 14 per cent as agricultural labourers, 3.34 per cent engaged in rearing livestock, forestry etc; and 5% in household industries and 8.08 per cent in other than household industries. Only 3.69 per cent are returned under trade and commerce, 10.37 per cent in construction, and the remaining 6.51 per cent are returned under various other services. (Singh K.S, 1993)

In Delhi, they are referred to as Gour Banjara and Sirkiband. Banjaras in Delhi are migrants from Rajstahan, Punjab and Uttar Pradesh; they also call themselves Rajput Banjaras. Their traditional occupation is trading. According to them, their main occupation was buying and selling of cattle by taking them to another place, but this has become a subsidiary trade for them. This subsidiary trade is also known as '*ladina lodna*'. The Banjaras of Delhi claim that with the introduction of railways and other modern means of transport, they wre forced to leave their traditional occupation and adopt a settled way of life which brought them face-to-face with the difficulties of earning a living from fixed occupations.

At present they are engaged as unskilled agricultural labourers, and in making *wattles* (sirkiband), and a few of them are engaged in peddling cosmetics. A number of them serve in government organisations, mainly the Delhi Electricity Supply Undertaking, Delhi Transport Corporation and Post and Telegraph Department in the capacity of mechanics, linesmen, drivers, peons and chowkidars. Some of them are engaged in the wholesale trading of wood, bamboo, ropes and other allied goods or in *wattle* making.

The poor send their children to work in tea-stalls, factories, vegetable shops, etc. to augment the family income. According to 1981 census, 27.81 per cent of them are returned as workers of them, 4 per cent are engaged in mining and quarrying, 3.01 per cent in household industries, 22.72 per cent in other than household industries, 16.48 per cent in construction activity, 13.38 per cent in trade and commerce, 6.88 percent in transport, storage and communication and the remaining 33.53 per cent in various other services.

ETHNOGRAPHIC PROFILE OF WADARS

(i) Population

According to Dr.Ambedkar Research and Training Institute, Pune, (1991) the estimated population of Wadars in Maharashta is 4.35 lakhs.

(ii) Geographical Distribution

Wadar community is one of the many Indian nomadic communities, known for their hard laborious work. Though they are found all over India, they are mainly concentrated in Andhra Pradesh, Maharashtra and Karnataka.

(iii) Origin

There is no exact idea about the origin of each culture. Therefore one has to depend upon the mythological and historical legendary stories. The legends are not exceptional regarding their origin. There are number of mythological and historical points contained in their legends.

Some of the Wadars claim that they are Kshatriyas. They believe that they are descendants of 'Bhagirath'. (Pt. Mahadevshashtri Joshi,). Given below are mythological narrations and evidences of the orgin of the community as perceived by them.

Mythological Evidence-1

As per the '*Rasmal*' scriptures, the muty regarding the origin of Wadars is as follows: Sidharaj, the King of Gujrat wanted to dig '*Sahastraling Lake*'. He brought Wadars from Malva to dig the lake. Jasma, was one of these Wadars, who was young and beautiful. She was a married woman. King Sidharaj fell in love with married Jasma. He requested her to come with him in the Palace, but she refused his request. She tried to run away when she got to know that she might be sexually exploited. King Sidharaj got angry and he followed her. He killed all those Wadars, who were trying to stop him, while he was following Jasma. At last, Jasma killed herself. But before dying she cursed the king that water will never get stored in the lake, for which he brought the Wadars to work. She told people of her caste that hereafter; women in Wadars will never be born beautiful. Furthermore she said, henceforth they should never apply hair oil and not to colour their eye-lashes (kajal). It is said that since that time Wadar women left the use of hair-oil and eye-lash makeup.

Mythological Evidence-2

The legend is about the traditional occupation of Wadars. Once upon a time king Oderaj was a ruler. He had a very beautiful Queen whose name was 'Balnagu'. Queen Balnagu was very beautiful. He had a son – 'Ramudi'. Once king had gone for hunting. Queen was standing by the door. The vagabond, who came to beg alms, saw the Queen and was taken up by her beauty. He kidnapped the Queen and carried her to his place of inhabitation which happened to be a cave. Queen had dropped pearls on the way while the vagabond was carrying her. When the king returned from hunting he didn't find the Queen at Palace, so he went out to find her. With the help of pearls dropped on the way by the Queen, he was able to find the cave of the vagabond who was a magician. His two brothers accompanied King. The vagabond had two magical sticks, with one of them, he used to convert the individuals into a stone, and with another stick, and he used to make them alive. With the first magical stick he converted all of them into stones, except the Queen. Ramudi, the son of King and Queen, who was brought up by his paternal aunt, came to know about his parents. He went into the cave of vagabond. He killed the vagabond and set his mother free. He found the magical sticks. With the help of the stick, he converted the three stones into human being.

After few years, Ramudi got married and became a king. After becoming a king he started using those two magical sticks.

He lost his mental balance. Whoever he saw he used to convert them into stones. He was trying to reach at Indra in heaven, by making the ladder of these stones. When Indra saw this, he got angry and pushed Ramudi, and also broke the stone ladder. At the same time Indra cursed him that his descendants will do the work of stone breaking. In the mean time, wives of the Ramudi's paternal uncles had removed glass bangles and they had also given up wearing the blouse (choli). Even today, the Wadar women do not wear the blouse in remembrance of that incidence. Hence till date the descendants of Ramudi are into stone-bearing business.

Mythological Evidence-3

According to this legend, Asalo and Kasalo were two brothers, who were the first males of Wadar caste. They were staying in Marwad, and came to Gujrat during the reign of King Sidharaj Jaysingh. Jehman was one of the daughters of the Prince Jaradan. King got his grand-daughter's married to Kasalo. On the death of Kasalo, Jehman jumps into the pier to complete the death rituals of 'sati'. Prince Jaradan built number of lakes, out of which the labourers, who were brought through the contact of Jehman, dug up 99 lakes. She received gold for this work. She sold this gold and used the money to take care of these labourers during famine. These labourers were forefathers of Wadars. Since then Wadars were involved in digging stone breaking, transporting and soil/clay related job.

(iv) Subcastes/Subgroups/Subtribes

There are three sub castes among the Wadars. These are: (1) Mati Wadar; (2) Jate Wadar (Fatare Wadar/Patharwat); (3) Gadi-Wadar.

(v) Clans

It is found that clans are same in all the above-mentioned three, sub castes of the Wadars. The clans are: Pawar, Shinde, Surve, Kurhade, Devkar, Jhakane (Zakne), Dhote, Masule, Phale, Rakhunde, Shirale, Jadhav, Kale, Orase, Chamkure, Kusalkar, Alkunte, Lashkare, Vikar, Mire, and Nalwade etc.

Marriage within the same clan is prohibited.

(vi) Dressing Pattern

The dress patterns of adult Wadar men and women Wadar are different than that and the youth of children. It is observed that Wadar men wear a dhoti – a white loin cloth which is tied around the waist like that of a Maharashtrian sari style. Their tops are known as *'bandi'*, which is like a sleeveless white cotton T-Shirt. Some of them wear white shirt also. The adult males often wear a Gandhi cap or white turban. The youth have taken upto wearing Trousers, shirts, T-shirts and modern clothes. The Wadar women on the other hand maintain the tradition they do not wear blouse but cover their breasts with the sari wrapped around their loins. There are legendary evidences and myths that explain why Wadar women don't wear blouse. Of let Wadar women, who have been influenced by urbanisation and modernisation had given up an idea of not wearing a blouse. In the rural areas we often come across the Wadar men and women in their traditional costumes.

(vii) Language/Dialect

The Wadars originally speaks *'Wadari'* dialect. The Wadars also speak Telgu, with each other, but can also manage to speak Kannad, Marathi and Hindi. However, while conducting fieldwork it was observed that the Wadar respondents said that they speak *'Wadri'* dialect. It was also observed that there are lot of Telgu, Kannada and very few Marathi words in the Wadri dialect. This probably hints at a clue of their original place, which is Andhra Pradesh. In Andhra Pradesh Wadars are known as *Wadrulu* or *Wadru*.

(viii) Traditional Occupation

There are different sub-castes among Wadars at different places, areas and regions. In Maharashtra there are three main sub-castes of the Wadars. Their nomenclature is very closely linked with the type of occupational responsibility, traditionally bestowed upon them.

The occupational responsibilities of Mati Wadars are digging up the soil, transporting the soil, including loading; unloading and finally using the soil for levelling up the grounds. The words '*mati*' in Marathi means 'soil' and hence occupation related to digging, transporting, loading and unloading of soil gave rise to the formation of name '*mati wadar*'.

The next sub-caste of the Wadars namly '*Jate Wadar*' has been derived from the '*Jate*' because its original meaning in Marathi is grinding stone. Since the traditional occupational responsibility of '*Jate Wadar*' was making grinding stones, hence they were referred to as '*Jate Wadars*'. According to Prabhakar Mande 'Jate Wadars', consider themselves higher than the *Mati* and *Gadi Wadars*, as they take pride in being artisans and creators of stone art work. The Jate Wadars have a tendency of nomadic movement as they move from one village to another and from one weekly market to another and from one fair to another for selling their products. When they are moving in the villages, they pitch their tents under a tree or near a temple or on the outskirts of the village, for a week or two. When the villagers come to know about the "*Jate Wadars*", they get their stone grinders, utensils and other gadgets and repairs or place an order for new ones.

The name of the third sub caste is derived from the word '*Gadi*' meaning cart or a vehicle, hence their traditional occupational responsibilities were breaking stones of the quarries, loading and unloading the same into a cart or a vehicle. According to Pandit Mahdevshastri Joshi the *Gadi* and *Mati Wadars* were not only associated with quarry work, but were involved in digging wells and doing small scale cultivation.

(ix) Food Habits

The staple diet of *Wadars* in Andhra Pradesh and Karnataka is rice and ragi and Jowar bread, whereas *Wadars* in Maharasthra prefer Jowar and *Bajara Bhakar* (bread). However, consumption of non-veg food such as beaf, pork, chicken, flesh of bandicoots and rats is common among the *Wadars*. (S.V. Ketkar, 1926) They also consume vegetables.

(x) Settlement

The traditional settlement pattern of the *Wadars* is known as '*Wadarwadi*'. The *Wadar* hamlet basically consists of 25 to 200 huts. In the rural areas these huts are made up of bamboo or stick walls with thatched roofes made up of leaves or rice-straw. In some villages the walls of *Wadar* houses are made up of clay or stones. Due to the demands of construction in Urban areas the demands of *Wadar* laboures increased, hence they come and settle either on the fringes of the cities near quarries or in slums. Their houses here are made up of tin or plastic sheet's walls. Some quarry owners provide them houses made up of brick and cement walls.

(xi) House Types

House types of *Wadars* vary. The houses given by quarry owners are strong, i.e. they are made up of brick or cement blocks or stones with Mangalore tiles, cement sheets or tin sheets as roofs. Those ones, who do not get a house from the employer, live in temporary tents made up of plastic sheets. The area of their tents is less than 100 sq. feet.

Traditional houses of the *Wadars* have thatched roof, stick, stone or clay walls. The shape of their houses is squarish or rectangular. They usually cook outside in the courtyard. Those *wadars* who have been absorbed into Government or private services or into construction business have build modern houses. Some of them are staying in apartments.

- **Family Pattern**

Both joint and nuclear family types are found among *Wadars*. As a nomadic community even if they may be living in separate huts as a nuclear families number of them also move in joint families, meaning a separate hut may be created for grand father/mother, son, their wife/children, paternal uncles etc. While conducting fieldwork, it was observed that nearly 15 to 30 members of joint family live near each other in separate tents, they may or may not be cooking on a separate hearth. Moving together provides them social, moral, mental and cultural support.

- **Marriage Pattern**

Although the marriage takes place at the brides place with the expenses of the bridegroom, a traditional pandal made up of gunny bags is erected. With the changes although some *Wadars* prefer to use the Hindu type of pandals, in a corner they still erect small pandal of gunny-bags. The bride's parents as well as groom's parents offer dinner or lunch to people from both the sides as a traditional norm. Earlier practice of serving food from both sides was there traditional organisation receive the money from the groom and with that money they give people uncooked foodgrains and pulses. The traditional political organisation used to maintain records of expenses incurred during the wedding, *Wadar* groom is allowed to get married to his parallel as well as cross cousins.

Traditionally *Wadars* never summoned a Brahmin priest to perform the wedding. An elderly person would perform the wedding. On the day prior to the wedding the bride's father with some of his close relatives go to the groom's village to ritually invite the party for the wedding. The groom's people worship the clan gods and apply five times sandle wood paste, first and turmeric power next on the forehead of the groom. The same ritual is repeated for the bride as well. On the next day, after the bath of the couple the groom holds of bride and takes her to "*pal*" a box-like structure made up of gunny bags use for transporting the bride. '*Fendlo*' means the wedding ritual goes on 2 to 3 days. The sequence of wedding ceremony begins with application of turmeric on the bodies of couple (Haldi), ritual bathing next day and actual wedding on the eve of the second day. On the third day leaves of Jamun and Mango are offered to Hanuman and a garland of Mango and Jamun trees are tied to sheeve of in the house. They consider them to be their clan gods. The ritual of taking around the Babhul branches, taking water, fetching is considered auspicious. The ritual of *Halad*, *Varat*, *Gangi Hoyar*, and *Mel-hoshad* are accompanied with songs sung by married women. The dialect of the songs is 'Wadri'. Maternal uncle brings the headgears (Bashing).

The practice of bride price that is to provide cash or kind to bride's father is very common among the Wadars. According to Pandit Mahadevshastri Joshi; wedding rituals of Kanade Wadars or Wardars from Karnataka and Andhra Pradesh vary from those of Maharashtra.

(xiv) Religious Practices

Wadars have several rituals and practices. Some of them are as follows:

(A) Birth Rituals

A woman who delivers restricts herself from cooking for a period for one month and 7 days. She is considered to be impure, after one month and 7 days, all the articles, furniture etc. in the house are cleaned with cow's urine with this ritual the woman who delivers a child become pure.

The ritual of doing '*Pachvi*' that is worshiping the goddess of fertility is done without fell. This ritual consists of applying oil to the child's mother, bathing her and filling her sari with stone grinder. This ceremony is called '*Oti Bharane*'. This ritual symbolizes the womb of the new mother.

The role of maternal uncle during the '*Barase* (child naming ceremony) is significant. He is supposed to buy new clothes for the new born. If there is no maternal uncle, proxy uncle is made to play this role.

Not much literature is available on the puberty rituals of Wadars.

(B) Death

The Wadar community buries dead bodies. Earlier, the soul migration ritual among the Wadars was observed on 3rd day after death of the person. This ritual is known as '*Dinum*'. The practices of preparing goat meat on soul migration are very common among the Wadars. This is done after six months of the death of the person.

According to Pt. Mahadevshastri Joshi, Wadars in Andhra Pradesh burry the dead bodies with their back facing the sun. On the third day, field mice and rice are boiled together and offered on the grave of dead person. The action of eating the food by crows symbolises the acceptance of the food by the soul of the dead. On the 10th day they offer meat to the birds. The practice of offering new clothes, food, chicken etc. to the ancestors on *Chaitra Padva*, '*Navratri*' is common among the Wadars of Karnataka.

(xv) Festivals

All the major festivals celebrated by the Hindus are observed by the Wadars. Some of these festivals are Diwali, Dassera, Holi, Sankrant, Navratri, etc. Some of the deiteis worshipped by them are *Khandoba ba*, *Kanhoba*, *Mhasoba*, *Sailanibaba*, *Sakladibaba*. Their main goddess is '*Mata*'. On the Dassera day the Wadars offer goat and chicken to the *Mata* (Goddess). They also worship the implements associated with their occupation on this day. The worship of ancestral sprits is very common among the Wadars. The images of '*Tak*' rectangular plates of brass, aluminum, etc. symbolise ancestral spirits.

Wadars from Karnataka are devotees of *Venkatesh*, *Marsoba*, *Mahadev*, *Maruti*, *Satwai*, *Murugavva*, *Nagamma*, and *Yellam*. They also go on pilgrim tours to Pandharpur, Tuljapur, and Tirupati etc.

(xvi) Folk-traditions

Body Tattooing

Body tattooing is common among Wadar women. Body tattooing is observed more among the women above the age of 35 years. It is observed that the Wadar women get their forearms tattooed. Traditionally some married women would get their backs, shoulders, necks and chests tattooed. Although the practice of tattooing among women is dying off, women compulsorily tattoo their forehead and, or chins. It is also observed that singing during wedding. Not much literature is available on the folk-traditions of the Wadars.

(xvii) Economic Condition

As mentioned earlier the Wadars are divided into three sub-castes namely *Jate Wadar*, *Mati Wadar* and *Gadi Wadar*. Out of the above mentioned three groups the economic conditions of those Gadi Wadars who have settled either in the slums or in better houses of metropolitan cities have progressed.

They have given up their traditional jobs of loading and unloading stones and taken up jobs in construction contractorship and in Government and Private sectors. The Mati and *Jete Wadars*, both in rural and urban areas are still coping up with progress, as they are poor as compared to the *Gadi Wadars*. This does not mean that all Gadi Wadars have progressed. Those poor *Gadi Wadars* in rural as well as urban areas are still victims of economic exploitation by the owners of unorganised sector or firms.

ETHNOGRAPHIC PROFILE OF BELDARS

(i) Population

According to Dr. Ambedkar Research and Training Institute, Pune (1991) the estimated population of Beldars in Maharashta is 1.85 lakhs.

(ii) Geographical Distribution

Our respondent revealed that the Beldars are distributed in drought prone district of Maharashtra. The respondents interviewed by us were from some of the drought prone areas of Maharashtra District.

(iii) Origin

According to Ramnath Chavan, there were some caste groups, which migrated from Rajasthan and nearby area and settled down in Maharashtra. In Maharashtra they started wondering for survival from one village to another. *'Beldar's* were one of these caste group. It is said that, during Mughal period, people of this community ran away from Rajasthan because of the threat of religious conversion.

(iv) Subcastes/Subgroups

According to Ramnath Chavan, *'Beldar'* is a main caste in which we found different sub-groups or subcastes. These subcastes are *Naik Beldar*, *Parmar Beldar*, *Od Rajput Beldar*, *Kumbhar Beldar* and *Gavandi Beldar*. The above-mentioned subgroups among the Beldars were identified specifically from their surnames and changed occupation.

(v) Clans

Clans found in Beldars are as follows: *Gondhale, Kudale, Chavan, Kate, Navale, Borade, Bhasati, Nivate, Ture,* and *Harade.* (Chavan Ramnath; 1996). During the fieldwork we found the clans namely *Mohite, Salunke.*

(vi) Dress Pattern

The Beldar women basically wear nine-yard saris in Maharashtra style. Young girls have taken up wearing salwar kamij. The men on the other hand wear shirt and trousers. Elderly men were seen wearing Dhoti and shirt. Some of them wear turban or Gandhi Cap.

(vii) Language/Dialect

Beldars in Maharashtra speak Marathi. Beldars originally belong to Rajasthan. Their mother tongue is Mewarie. Since last 400 to 500 years, they have settled in Maharashtra and hence speak 'Marathi' the regional language.

(viii) Traditional Occupation

There were some caste-groups, which migrated from Rajasthan and nearby area, and settled down in Maharashtra-'Beldar community' was one of them. During Mughal period, people of this community ran away from Rajasthan because of threat of religious conversion. Before Mughal period, Beldars were bodyguards of the Kings. They were also in the army. They used to make tools/implements required for the war and also to provide security to the Palace. These were their main occupations. At the same time they were also expert in designing and sculpture. (Chavan Ramnath; 1996)

According to Ramnath Chavan, Beldars who migrated to Maharashtra, opted different occupations for survival in different cities of Maharashtra. In some villages it is found that they carry the soil stones on the back of donkeys from one place to another. Besides this they also make stone gadgets like grinding stone, pounder etc.

Since last some years, the Beldars who working/labouring on road-construction or building construction. A few of them are now settled as building contractors. Some of them are in the business of transportation of construction material. Nearly 50 per cent people of the Beldar community do the soil related work. These people call themselves as *'Gavandi'*. *'Gavandi'* is Marathi word for *'masson'*. Members of this caste also work as brick kiln owners, small-scale businessmen motor mechanics, carpenters, etc.

(ix) Food Habits

The staple diet of Beldars includes rice, jowar and bajara bread, chapattis; they also consume pulses like toor, gram, udid etc. and vegetables.

(x) Settlement Pattern

Traditional settlement patterns of Beldars in Ahamadnagar are known by term Beldar Vastis or Wadas. These settlements comprise of 10 to 50 houses.

(xi) House Types

House types of Beldars vary. During fieldwork it was observed that quarry-owner has provided houses to them. The houses are made up of bricks or cement blocks or stones with tin sheets, cement sheets as roof. Sometimes the houses are with tin sheets walls and tin sheets or plastic sheets as roof. The area of the houses is between the ranges of 100 to 150 sq.ft.

(xii) Family Pattern

Both joint and nuclear family types are found among Beldars. While conducting fieldwork it was observed that close relatives of the Beldars live near each other, but in separate houses. They cook separately. Moving together from one quarry to another provides them social, moral, mental and cultural support.

(xiii) Marriage Pattern

According to Ramnath Chavan and Uttam Kamble marriage within sub castes is not allowed among Beldars.

Beldars give importance to the 'Gotra' i.e. clans. Cross-cousin marriage is not allowed. The engagement ceremony of the Beldars known as '*Sagai*'.

When people from bridegroom's party go for '*sagai*', they have to carry blocks of brown sugare. For '*Sagai*' they call '*jat-panchayat*'. Then they break 'the jaggery block into small pieces, and keep the pieces on the palms of the people who have came for '*Sagai*'. Then they start discussing on various issues e.g. Is there any disorder physical or mental problem of bride or bridegroom?, whether bride or bridegroom is already married, is community has expelled the family of bride or groom?. If nobody objects or any question does not arise then the piece of jaggery is thrown by turning the palm down. The beldars believe unless and until they do not find solution to a given problem, they cannot turn down the Jaggery place from the palm. Among Beldars the bridegroom gives bride price to the bride, which is called as '*Dahej*'. The bride price varies from Rs. 11 to Rs. 51. Besides this, bridegroom has to give clothes to bride and her parents. Marriage goes on for three days. On the first day the ritual of application of turmeric paste (*Halad*) on the bodies of couple (i.e. bride and bridegroom) takes place. On second day they perform a ritual of removing the turmeric.

On last day i.e. third day marriage ceremony takes place. Marriage rituals are similar with the rituals of Hindu marriage. On the wedding day, for lunch or dinner as a norm only non-vegetarian food, must be served. Serving sweet food is a taboo.

Bledar woman do not get divorce. Husband and wife have to take up the matter to the traditional political organisation, if divorce is must.

Widow marriage is not allowed among Beldars. A man is allowed to marry more than once, but with the permission of his first wife. Child-marriage is not allowed among Beldars.

(xiv) Religious Practices

Beldars are basically Hindus and hence they worship almost all the Hindu deities.

(xv) Festivals

Major Hindu festivals such as *Diwali, Dasshera, Makar Sankranti, Rakhi-purnima, Holi*, and *Rangpanchmi* etc. are celebrated prevalent among the Beldars. Patriarchy, patriling and patrilocal residency is the cultural norm.

(xvi) Economic Background

Beldars are economically backward. Most of them are daily wage labourers, as most of them do not have financial assets and resources to bank on. They are mostly found to be semi-nomadic. This is due to lack of job opportunities back home in rural area.

ETHNOGRAPHIC PROFILE OF THE TIRUMALS

(i) Brief Introduction

Out of the two stone quarry sites studied, Yewalewadi did not have any Tirmul families, however in Moshi, we did come across a few of them. These families have been working as stone quarry labourers since 15 to 20 years. There was hardly any secondary literature available on the Community. An attempt was made to search Internet websites in order to avail information on the Tirumals, but our efforts were fulfill. Using Focus Group Discussion method, were tried to get few details about the group. One of the limitations which came across was the male-folk used to be drunk on "Sundays" –i.e. their holiday. The women-folk would co-operate by giving some information. Thus, the ethnographic details in this section are not comprehensive.

(ii) Origin

The Tirumals of Moshi claim that they are original inhabitants of Tirupathy in the southern state of Andhra Pradesh. They say that they have migrated to Maharashtra in search of jobs.

(iii) Dialect

They say they speak Telgu, but after living in Maharashtra for last 15 years, they can speak Marathi and Hindi fluently.

(iv) Geographical Distribution

As mentioned earlier, the Tirumals are found in and around Tirupathy in the state of Andhra Pradesh.

(v) Traditional Occupation

Tirumal respondents interviewed said that their traditional occupation was to perform death rituals and do mental jobs related to death rites. They were, hence looked down upon by the upper castes.

(vi) Forms of Marriage

Monogamy is the major form of marriage, however polygyny is allowed if the man promises to take care of other wives.

(vii) Family Types

Both nuclear and joint families are and bamboo stick walls and thatched roofs. The shape of the house is rectangular and the size is 200 to 400 square feet.

(viii) Religion

Tirumals are basically Hindus and hence they worship almost all the Hindu deities. Some of the Tirumals we interviewed said that Tirupathy Balaji is worshipped most often.

(ix) Festivals

Major Hindu Festivals such as Diwali, Dasshera, Sankarant, Rakhi Pornima, and Holi etc. are celebrated prevalent among the Tirumals. Patriarchy, patriling and patrilocal residency are the cultural norms.

(x) Settlement Pattern

Traditional settlement pattern of the Tirumals comprise of 25 to 200 houses. The locations of the Tirumal settlements were mostly on the outskirts of a village, as they were considered to untouchables once upon a time.

(xi) House Types

Traditional Tirumal houses are made up of clay walls or palm leaf by the Tirumals. They consider Tirupathy Balaji as their pilgrimage centre.

(xii) Changes

Tirumals who were socially degraded and stigmatised due to their caste status. Most of them were landless and did not have any financial resources, as a result of which they were hand to mouth. This status force them to migrate to cities of Andhra Pradesh and other states including Maharashtra to work as daily wage labourers in unorganised sectors. They have become victims of the owners of private unorganised firms, where the tentades of insecurity, bonded labour and exploitation have choked them. Their lives revolve around their employers for livelihood and hence the show is on.

4

SOCIO-ECONOMIC STATUS OF STONE QUARRY WORKERS

SOCIO-ECONOMIC STATUS OF TARGET POPULATION

A society is a complex structure of various groups and classes. These groups behave according to expectations and norms of the society. There are different norms prescribed for the behaviour of different members of the society. For example, a boy behaves differently as compared to a girl. There is a condition in the society in which various constituent parts discharge different functions in relation to quality as a result of which it is possible to achieve social objectives. In the interest of organisation different members are placed in different positions. This replacement is generally speaking called status and the functions that are connected with the status or the functions that are connected with the discharge being the member of a particular status is called 'role'. Every member has status in the society, but it does not mean that he has only one status. (Singh K., 1989; 310).

While classifying the characteristics of the term 'status', Singh K. (1989; 311) stated that status is determined by: (1) the cultural situation of a particular society; (2) it is determined only in relevance of the other members in society; (3) every individual has to play certain role in accordance with this status; (4) status is the only part of whole society; (5) it carries prestige with it; (6) status is categorised by sociologist into two categories namely: (i) achieved status – the position that a person earns out of his own efforts; (ii) ascribed status – it is given to song on the basis of the situation in the society or by the other members of the society. For example the ascribed status is based on the indicators such as age, sex, kinship, caste, race, family etc. whereas achieved status is based on personal abilities such as education, earned wealth, popularity etc. Sociologists have defined the corelation between status, role and power.

Since the target population of the present study are stone-quarry workers belonging to the nomadic caste groups such as Wadar, Laman, Beldar and Tirumal. It is interesting to note that these groups have been traditionally associated with caste occupations, which according to caste system norms are determined by birth. All the above-mentioned communities have been working as stone-workers, stonebreakers, artisans, transporters etc. in according to the traditional caste system norms.

Historical and written evidences on these groups definitely associate them some or the other kind of work related to stones. Various Kings and Kingdoms have constantly invaded India. The Kings and Emperors who ruled India were aware of these stone-worker communities and from time to time use them for creation of art, scriptures, building, monuments, forts and other heritage sites. For example, the forts in Maharashtra made up of stones are handy work of the Wadar community. Forts in Andhra Pradesh built by the Nizams were the handy works of the Lamans and the Wadru community in the State. Similarly, there was a time in the past where technology had not been developed, it was during that time stone-workers such as Wadars and Beldars made stone-grinders and other kitchen utensils. The Mati-Wadars and the Lamans use their donkeys to transport soil and other construction material, however after Independence when India became free from British rule, the first Prime Minister and his Government led emphasis on technological development and industrialisation. The rise of this movement was the beginning of the setback for artisans and caste-groups, which were into traditional technological business using low cost and primitive technologies.

With the rise of modernisation, urbanisation and new technology there was rapid shift in the social and economic structures of occupation based caste-groups. There was a time when the stone-workers used big and small hammers to break stones, but as time pass by the technology of blasting big rocks came in along with stone crushing machines, which minimised and cut down manual labour.

On one hand India witnessed rapid technological changes especially in and on the fringes of the cities where prevailed the process of modernisation and urbanisation, whereas on the other hand majority of caste communities associated with the stone work in the rural areas still continued serving the rural masses and gaining less money for their services as there was no demand for their handy work without technological support in the cities. For example, mixers, juicers have replaced stone-grinders, as they are quick and easy to work with. The introduction of these electronic gadgets naturally reduced the cost of manually made stone-gadgets. This process also hampered the income process and the self-employment status of the traditional caste stone-working community.

Unemployment and lack of demand of stone art and craft forced these caste-groups to migrate to cities, outskirts of the cities and to the stone-quarries as cheap labourers. The stone-quarry owners took advantage of the situations and the struggles faced by these poor communities most of who were nomads and semi-nomads. Secondly, most of these groups were not into full time cultivation and hence did not settle in one place although the study has revealed that some of the stone-quarry workers do own agriculture land, but whatever is produced is mostly for consumption of the family. This chapter hence deals with both the ascribed as well as the achieved status of the Wadars, Lamans, Beldars and Tirumals.

SOCIAL STATUS

Caste-wise Break-up of Respondents

Table 4.1 shows that the respondents belong to four caste-groups namely Wadars, Lamans, Beldars and Tirumals. Table also depicts caste-wise break-up of the respondents. Out of 150 respondents, 62 i.e. 41.3 per cent respondents belong to Wadar caste; 51 i.e. 34 per cent respondents belong to Lamani caste; 32 i.e.21 per cent respondents are Beldars and remaining 5 i.e. 3.3 per cent respondents belong to Tirumal caste.

Table 4.1

Caste-wise break-up of respondents

Sr. No.	*Caste*	*Number*	*Percentage*
1.	Wadars	62	41.3
2.	Lamans	51	34
3.	Beldars	32	21
4.	Tirumal	05	3.3
	Total	**150**	**100**

All the above communities have been traditionally associated with stonework. They have been giving services associated with their profession to other caste groups. With the rising demand for construction in the cities and towns these groups find employment at the stone quarries.

Sex-wise Break-up of Respondents

Table 4.2 depicts sex-wise break-up of the respondents. Out of 150 respondents 133 i.e. 89 per cent respondents are males while 17 i.e. 11 per cent respondents are females.

Table 4.2

Sex-wise break-up of respondents

Sr. No.	*Caste*	*Number*	*Percentage*
1.	Males	133	89
2.	Females	17	11
	Total	**150**	**100**

The high percentage of males coming forward to speak to the researcher indicates that the women-folk still do not want to interact freely.

Sex-wise Break-up of Wadar Respondents

Table 4.3 shows sex-wise break-up of the Wadar respondents. Out of 62 Wadar respondents, 57 i.e. 92 per cent respondents are males while only 5 i.e. 8per cent respondents are females.

Out of total 133 (89%) male respondents, Wadar males are 43 per cent while out of total 17 (11%) female respondents Wadar females are 29.4 per cent.

Table 4.3

Sex-wise break-up of Wadar respondents

Sr. No.	*Caste*	*Number*	*Percentage*
1.	Males	57	92
2.	Females	5	8
	Total	**62**	**100**

Sex-wise break-up of Laman Respondents

Table 4.4 shows sex-wise break-up of the Laman respondents. Out of 51 Laman respondents, 45 i.e. 88 per cent respondents are males while 6 i.e. 12 per cent respondents are females.

Out of total 133 (89%) male respondents Laman males are 34 per cent and out of total 17 (11%) female respondents Laman female are 35.2 per cent.

Table 4.4

Sex-wise break-up of Laman respondents

Sr. No.	*Caste*	*Number*	*Percentage*
1.	Males	45	88
2.	Females	6	12
	Total	**51**	**100**

Here again the percentage of male Laman respondents is high.

Sex-wise Break-up of Beldar Respondents

Table 4.5 shows sex-wise break-up of Beldar respondents. It is evident from the table 4.5 that out of 32 Beldar respondents 26 i.e. 81 per cent are male respondents while 6 i.e. 19 per cent respondents are females.

Out of total 133 (89%) male respondents, 19 per cent are Beldar males while out of total 17 (11%) female respondents 35.2 per cent are Beldar females.

Table 4.5

Sex-wise Break-up of Beldar Respondents

Sr. No.	*Caste*	*Number*	*Percentage*
1.	Males	26	81
2.	Females	6	19
	Total	**32**	**100**

Sex-wise Break-up of Tirumals

It is observed that out of five Tirumal respondents, all 5 respondents are males, and out of total 133 (89%) male respondents Tirumal males are 4 per cent. While searching the stone quarry communities it was observed that maximum workers are from Wadar and Laman communities, followed by Beldars. However, we came across the Tirumals, who claim to have migrated from Andhra Pradesh. Their traditional occupation according to them was associated with death and soul migration ritual. They are looked down upon due to this stigma, in Andhra Pradesh. At Moshi quarry sites we came across this community. An attempt is made to highlight their socio-economic background as well.

Age-range of the Respondents

From Table 4.6 it is evident that maximum number of respondents i.e. 78 (52%) out of 150 respondents are within the age-range of 18 to 30 years, followed by 37 i.e. 25 per cent respondents out of 150 respondents within the age-range of 30 to 40 years. Out of 150 respondent, 14 i.e. 9 per cent of respondents are between the age-range of 40 to 50 years; 9 i.e. 6 per cent of respondents are within 50 to 60 years of age-range and 7 i.e. 5 per cent of them are above 60 year of age. Remaining 5 i.e. 3 per cent respondents are up to 18 years of age.

Table 4.6

Age range of respondents

Sr. No.	*Age range*	*Number*	*Percentage*
1.	Upto 18 yrs.	5	3
2.	18 yrs. to 30 yrs.	78	52
3.	30 yrs. to 40 yrs.	37	25
4.	40 yrs. to 50 yrs.	14	9
5.	50 yrs. to 60 yrs.	9	6
6.	Above 60 yrs.	7	5
	Total	**150**	**100**

The table certainly reveals that maximum labourers and workers are from 18 to 40 years category, i.e. 77 per cent. Only the young and middle aged (up to 40 years) can handle quarry type of jobs.

Age-range of Wadar Respondents

Table 4.7 depicts the age-range of Wadar respondents. It is evident from the Table 4.7 that 30 i.e. 48 per cent of respondents, out of 62 Wadar respondents are within the age-range of 18 to 30 years, followed by 14 i.e. 23 per cent respondents who are within the age-range of 30 to 40 years. Out of 62 respondents 5 i.e. 8 per cent are within 40 to 50 years of age-range of 50 to 60 years and 6 i.e. 10 per cent respondents are above 60 years of age.

Table 4.7

Age-range of Wadar respondents

Sr. No.	Age range	Number	Percentage
1.	Upto 18 yrs.	0	0
2.	18 yrs. to 30 yrs.	30	48
3.	30 yrs. to 40 yrs.	14	23
4.	40 yrs. to 50 yrs.	5	8
5.	50 yrs. to 60 yrs.	7	11
6.	Above 60 yrs.	6	10
	Total	**62**	**100**

As mentioned in Table 4.6 that maximum labourers and workers are in the age range category of 18 to 40 years. Table 4.7 too reveals that 71 per cent of the Wadar respondents are in the same age range category.

Age-range of Laman Respondents

Table No. 4.8 depicts the age-range of Laman respondents. The table reveals that out of 51 Laman respondents 31 (61%) are between the age-range of 18 to 30 years, 7 (14%) respondents are up to the 18 years of age, 6 i.e. 11 per cent respondents are within the age-range of 30 to 40 years. 4 i.e. 8 per cent respondents, out of 51, are within the age-range of 40 to 60 years; 2 (4%) are between 50 to 60 years and 1 (2%) respondent is above 60 years of age.

Table 4.8

Age-range of Laman Respondents

Sr. No.	Age range	Number	Percentage
1.	Upto 18 yrs.	7	14
2.	18 yrs. to 30 yrs.	31	61
3.	30 yrs. to 40 yrs.	6	11
4.	40 yrs. to 50 yrs.	4	8
5.	50 yrs. to 60 yrs.	2	4
6.	Above 60 yrs.	1	2
	Total	**51**	**100**

Even among the Laman respondents the percentage of labourers and workers is as high as 72 per cent, between the age range 18 to 40 years.

Age-range of Beldar Respondents

Table 4.9 shows the age-range of Beldar respondents. As evident from the Table 4.9, 15 i.e. 47 per cent respondents, out of 32 Beldar respondents, are within the age-range of 18 to 30 years, 12 i.e. 37 per cent of them are between the age-range of 30 to 40 years; while remaining 5 i.e. 16 per cent respondents are within the age-range of 40 to 50 years.

Table 4.9

Age-range of Beldar respondents

Sr. No.	*Age range*	*Number*	*Percentage*
1.	Up to 18 yrs.	0	0
2.	18 yrs. To 30 yrs.	15	47
3.	30 yrs. To 40 yrs.	12	37
4.	40 yrs. To 50 yrs.	5	16
5.	50 yrs. To 60 yrs.	0	0
6.	Above 60 yrs.	0	0
	Total	**32**	**100**

Beldar respondents too show the same trait of 84 per cent of labourers and respondents between the age range 18 to 40 years.

Age of Tirumal Respondents

Out of 5 Tirumal respondents, it is observed that 4 i.e. 80 per cent respondents are between the age-range of 18 to 30 years. While 1 (i.e. 20%) respondent is between the age-range of 30 to 40 years

Interestingly 100 per cent of the Tirumal respondents are between the age range of 18 to 40 years. Hence, it could be concluded that hard manual work and young age goes together. It is certainly not a cup of tea of old people.

Marital Status of Respondents

From Table 4.10 it is evident that 138 i.e. 92 per cent respondents, out of 150, are married, 7 i.e. 5 per cent are single or unmarried, 3 i.e.. 2 per cent of them are separated, 2 i.e. 1 per cent of the respondents are widows while remaining 1 (0.7%) respondent is widower.

Table 4.10

Marital status of respondents

Sr. No.	*Marital status*	*Number*	*Percentage*
1.	Unmarried	7	5
2.	Married	138	92
3.	Widow	2	1
4.	Widower	1	0.7
5.	Separated	2	1
6.	Divorcee	0	0
7.	Others	0	0
	Total	**150**	**100**

Table 4.10 shows that as many as 91 of the respondents are married.

Marital Status of Wadars

Table 4.11 given below shows marital status of Wadar respondents. Out of 62 Wadar respondents 59 i.e. 95 of the respondents are married while remaining 3 i.e. 5 respondents are widow, widower and separated.

Among the Wadars too, the percentage of married respondents is as high as 95.

Marital Status of Lamans

It is evident from Table 4.12 that out of 51 Laman respondents, 43 i.e. 84 per cent respondents are married, 7 i.e. 14 per cent are single or unmarried while remaining one i.e. 2 per cent respondent is widow.

Table 4.11

Marital status of Wadar respondents

Sr. No.	*Marital status*	*Number*	*Percentage*
1.	Unmarried	0	0
2.	Married	59	95
3.	Widow	1	1.6
4.	Widower	1	1.6
5.	Separated	1	1.6
6.	Divorcee	0	0
7.	Others	0	0
	Total	**62**	**100**

Table 4.12

Marital status of Laman respondents

Sr. No.	*Marital status*	*Number*	*Percentage*
1.	Unmarried	7	14
2.	Married	43	84
3.	Widow	1	2
4.	Widower	0	0
5.	Separated	0	0
6.	Divorcee	0	0
7.	Others	0	0
	Total	**51**	**100**

The same trend of high percentage of marriage is seen among the Lamans.

Marital Status of Beldars

Table 4.13 shows marital status of Beldars. Out of 32 Beldar respondents, 31 i.e. 97 respondents are married while only one i.e. 3 respondent is separated.

Table 4.13

Marital status of Beldar respondents

Sr. No.	*Marital status*	*Number*	*Percentage*
1.	Unmarried	0	0
2.	Married	31	97
3.	Widow	0	0
4.	Widower	0	0
5.	Separated	1	3
6.	Divorcee	0	0
7.	Others	0	0
	Total	**32**	**100**

Marital Status of Tirumals

Table 4.14 shows marital status of Tirumal respondents. It is evident from the table that all 5 i.e. 100 per cent of the respondents are married.

Table 4.14

Marital status of Tirumals

Sr. No.	*Marital status*	*Number*	*Percentage*
1.	Unmarried	0	0
2.	Married	5	100
3.	Widow	0	0
4.	Widower	0	0
5.	Separated	0	0
6.	Divorcee	0	0
7.	Others	0	0
	Total	**5**	**100**

Mother Tongue of Respondents

Table 4.15 reflects on mother tongue of the respondents. From the table given below it is evident that the mother tongue of 62 i.e. 41.3 per cent respondents is 'Wadri' i.e. all Wadar respondents speak 'Wadri' dialect, but they can also speak Marathi, Hindi and Telgu language. Out of 150, 51 i.e. 34 per cent of the respondent speak Lamani. The mothertongue of 32 i.e. 21 per cent respondents is Marathi, these are the Beldar respondents. Mother tongue of Tirumal respondents is Telgu and their number is 5 i.e. 3.3 per cent of the total respondents.

Table 4.15

Mother tonge of respondents

Sr. No.	Mother tongue	Number	Percentage
1.	Wadri (Wadars)	62	41.3
2.	Lamani (Lamans)	51	34
3.	Marathi (Beldars)	32	21
4.	Telgu (Tirumal)	5	3.3
	Total	**150**	**100**

Family Size

Table 4.16 reflects on family size of the respondents. It is evident from the Table 4.16 that 82 i.e. 55 per cent of the respondents, out of 150, have the family size between 1 to 4 members, 60 i.e. 40 per cent respondents have the family size between 4 to 6 members while remaining 8 i.e. 5 per cent of the respondents have their family size up to 8 members.

Table 4.16

Family size

Sr. No.	Family size	Number	Percentage
1.	1 to 4	82	55
2.	4 to 6	60	40
3.	6 to 8	8	5
4.	Above 8	0	0
	Total	**150**	**100**

Family Size of Wadars

It is evident from the Table 4.17 that out of 62 Wadar respondents, 37 i.e. 60 per cent of the respondents have their family size between 1 to 4 members, 18 i.e. 29 per cent of the respondents have their family size up to 6 members while 7 i.e. 11 per cent of the respondents have their family size up to 8 members.

Table 4.17

Family size of Wadars

Sr. No.	*Family size*	*Number*	*Percentage*
1.	1 to 4	37	60
2.	4 to 6	18	29
3.	6 to 8	7	11
4.	Above 8	0	0
	Total	**62**	**100**

Family Size of Lamans

Table 4.18 depicts family size of Laman respondents. Out of 51 Laman respondents 30 i.e. 59 per cent of the respondents have family size between 1 to 4 members, 20 i.e. 39 per cent of them have family size 4 to 6 members; while only one respondent (2%) has the family size between 6 to 8 members.

Table 4.18

Family size of Lamans

Sr. No.	*Family size*	*Number*	*Percentage*
1.	1 to 4	30	59
2.	4 to 6	20	39
3.	6 to 8	1	2
4.	Above 8	0	0
	Total	**51**	**100**

Family Size of Beldars

From the Table 4.19 it is evident that out of 32 Beldar respondents, 14 i.e. 44 per cent of the respondents have their family size between 1 to 4 members; while 18 i.e. 56 per cent of them have their family size between 4 to 6 members.

Table 4.19

Family size of Beldars

Sr. No.	*Family size*	*Number*	*Percentage*
1.	1 to 4	14	44
2.	4 to 6	18	56
3.	6 to 8	0	0
4.	Above 8	0	0
	Total	**32**	**100**

Family Size of Tirumals

Table No. 4.20 depicts family size of Tirumal respondents. Out of 5 Tirumal respondents 2 i.e. 40 per cent respondents have their family size between 1 to 4 members; while remaining 5 i.e. 60 per cent respondents have their family size between 4 to 6 members.

Table 4.20

Family size of Tirumals

Sr. No.	*Family size*	*Number*	*Percentage*
1.	1 to 4	2	40
2.	4 to 6	3	60
3.	6 to 8	0	0
4.	Above 8	0	0
	Total	**5**	**100**

EDUCATIONAL STATUS

Educational Status of Respondents

Table 4.21 reflects educational status of the respondents. From the given table it is seen that maximum number of respondents i.e. 102 means 68 per cent respondents, out of 150 respondents, are illiterate; 15 i.e. 10 per cent of them educated up to primary level and 25 i.e. 17 per cent of the respondents educated up to secondary level. 6 i.e. 4 per cent of the respondents educated up to higher secondary level; while one respondent (0.7%) is graduate and remaining one respondent (0.7%) is post-graduate.

Table 4.21

Educational status of respondent

Sr. No.	*Educational status*	*Number*	*Percentage*
1.	Illiterate	102	68
2.	Primary	15	10
3.	Secondary	25	17
4.	Higher Secondary	6	4
5.	Graduate	1	0.7
6.	Post-graduate	1	0.7
7.	Others	0	0
	Total	**150**	**100**

Overall illiteracy rate among the stone quarry workers is as high as 68 per cent, with 83 per cent for males and 17 per cent among females.

Educational Status of Spouse of Respondents

Table 4.22 depicts the educational status of spouse of respondents. From table given below it is seen that out of 150 respondents 12 i.e. 8 per cent respondents are unmarried; i.e. they are without their spouse, hence the question of these 12 respondents does not arise, while some are either widow or widowers. 115 i.e. 77 per cent of the spouses of the respondents are illiterate, 5 i.e. 3 per cent of the spouses are educated up to primary level; while 18 i.e. 12 per cent of them are educated up to secondary level.

Table 4.22

Educational status of spouses of respondents

Sr. No.	*Educational status*	*Number*	*Percentage*
1.	Illiterate	115	77
2.	Primary	5	3
3.	Secondary	18	12
4.	Higher Secondary	0	0
5.	Graduate	0	0
6.	Post-graduate	0	0
7.	N.A.	12	8
	Total	**150**	**100**

Educational Status of Wadar Respondents

Table 4.23 reflects that out of 62 Wadar respondents, 48 i.e. 77 per cent respondents are illiterate; 10 i.e. 16 per cent of the respondents are educated up to primary level, while 3 i.e. 5 per cent of them have got education up to secondary level and only one respondent (2%) is educated up to higher secondary level.

Table 4.23

Educational status of Wadar respondents

Sr. No.	*Educational status*	*Number*	*Percentage*
1.	Illiterate	48	77
2.	Primary	10	16
3.	Secondary	3	5
4.	Higher Secondary	1	2
5.	Graduate	0	0
6.	Post-graduate	0	0
7.	Others	0	0
	Total	**62**	**100**

Illiteracy rate among Wadars too is 77 per cent, with 69 per cent among males and 8 per cent among females.

Educational Status of Spouses of Wadar Respondents

Educational status of spouse of Wadar respondents is given in Table 4.24. The table reflects that out of 62 Wadar respondents, 3 respondents (i.e. 5%) are not applicable to this question/ indicator, remaining 59 spouses of 59 respondents (i.e. 95% spouses) are illiterate i.e. not single spouse of the Wadar respondents is educated.

Table 4.24

Educational status of spouses of Wadar respondents

Sr. No.	*Educational status*	*Number*	*Percentage*
1.	Illiterate	59	100
2.	Primary	0	0
3.	Secondary	0	0
4.	Higher Secondary	0	0
5.	Graduate	0	0
6.	Post-graduate	0	0
7.	Others	0	0
	Total	**59**	**100**

The spouses of Wadar respondents mostly females show 100% illiteracy status.

Educational Status of Laman Respondents

Table 4.25 depicts educational status of Laman respondents. From the table, it is evident that out of 51 Laman respondents 34 i.e. 67 per cent of the respondents are illiterate; 4 i.e. 8 per cent of them are educated up to primary level; 12 i.e. 23 per cent of the respondents have got education up to secondary level; while remaining one respondent (2%) is educated up to higher secondary level i.e. up to XIIth grade.

Table 4.25

Educational status of Laman respondents

Sr. No.	*Educational status*	*Number*	*Percentage*
1.	Illiterate	34	67
2.	Primary	4	8
3.	Secondary	12	23
4.	Higher Secondary	1	2
5.	Graduate	0	0
6.	Post-graduate	0	0
7.	Others	0	0
	Total	**51**	**100**

The trend of illiteracy among the Laman respondents is 67 per cent.

Educational Status of Spouses of Laman Respondents

Table 4.26 shows the educational status of spouses of Laman respondents. From the table given below, it is seen that out of 51 Laman respondents 8 i.e. 16 per cent of the respondents are unmarried are without spouses. Hence the question of educational status of these 8 unmarried respondents does not arise. Among remaining 43 spouses, 38 i.e. 74 per cent spouse of respondents are illiterate; 2 i.e. 4 per cent of the spouses are educated up to primary level; while 3 i.e. 6 per cent of them have got education up to secondary level.

Table 4.26

Educational status of spouses of Laman respondents

Sr. No.	*Educational status*	*Number*	*Percentage*
1.	Illiterate	38	74
2.	Primary	2	4
3.	Secondary	3	6
4.	Higher Secondary	0	0
5.	Graduate	0	0
6.	Post-graduate	0	0
7.	Others	0	0
8.	N.A.	8	16
	Total	**51**	**100**

Illiteracy rate among the spouses of Laman respondents too is 74 per cent.

Educational Status of Beldar respondents

The Table 4.27 given below shows that out of 32 Beldar respondents, 18 i.e. 56.3 per cent of the Beldar respondents are illiterate; one (i.e. 3%) is educated up to primary level; 8 i.e. 25 per cent of them are educated up to secondary level and 3 i.e. 9.4 per cent of them are educated up to higher secondary level. Out of remaining two respondents, one is graduate and the other one has completed his post-graduation.

Table 4.27

Educational status of Beldar respondents

Sr. No.	*Educational status*	*Number*	*Percentage*
1.	Illiterate	18	56.3
2.	Primary	1	3
3.	Secondary	8	25
4.	Higher Secondary	3	9.4
5.	Graduate	1	3
6.	Post-graduate	1	3
7.	Others	0	0
	Total	32	100

Illiteracy percentage of Beldar respondents is 56.3 per cent.

Educational Status of Spouses of Beldar Respondents

From Table 4.28 it is evident that out of 32 spouses of the respondents, 16 means 50 per cent of the spouses are illiterate; 3 i.e. 9 per cent of them are educated up to primary level and 13 i.e. 41 per cent of the spouses have got education up to secondary level.

Table 4.28

Educational status of spouses of Beldar respondents

Sr. No.	*Educational status*	*Number*	*Percentage*
1.	Illiterate	16	50%
2.	Primary	3	9%
3.	Secondary	13	41%
4.	Higher Secondary	0	0
5.	Graduate	0	0
6.	Post-graduate	0	0
7.	Others	0	0
	Total	**32**	**100%**

The illiteracy percentage among the spouses of Beldar respondents is 50 per cent, comparatively better.

Educational Status of Tirumal Respondents

Table 4.29 depicts educational status of Tirumal respondents as well as their spouse. Out of 5 Tirumal respondents (Ego) two respondents (40%) are illiterate; two of them (40%) are educated up to secondary level while only one respondent (20%) is educated up to higher secondary level. Out of 5 spouses of Tirumal respondents, 3 i.e. 60 per cent are illiterate; while 2 of them have got education up to secondary level.

Table 4.29

Educational status of Tirumal respondents and their spouse

Sr. No.	*Educational status*	*Ego*		*Ego's spouse*	
		Number	*Percentage*	*Number*	*Percentage*
1.	Illiterate	2	40	3	60
2.	Primary	0	0	0	0
3.	Secondary	2	40	2	40
4.	Higher Secondary	1	20	0	0
5.	Graduate	0	0	0	0
6.	Post-graduate	0	0	0	0
7.	Others	0	0	0	0
	Total	**5**	**100**	**5**	**100**

ECONOMIC STATUS

Occupational Status of the Respondents (ego)

Table 4.30 depicts occupational status of the respondents. There are different types of jobs exist among stone quarry workers like big stone breaking, small stones breaking, loading the trucks, machine operators, supervisors, tar-labourers etc.

Table 4.30

Occupational status of respondents

Sr. No.	*Occupation*	*Number*	*Percentage*
1.	Big stone breaking	83	49
2.	Breaking small stones	21	12
3.	Loading	18	11
4.	Driving	22	13
5.	Machine operator	5	3
6.	Tar labourers	6	4
7.	Supervisors	6	4
8.	Contractor	2	1
9.	Cleaner	1	0.6
10.	Housewife	1	2.06
11.	Others	3	2
	Total	**168**	**100**

From Table 4.30 it is clear that 72 per cent of the stone quarry workers are unskilled labourers, hence the degree of social, economic, educational, health and housing insecurity is high.

From the Table 4.30 it is evident that out of 168, 83 i.e. 49 per cent of the respondents do the work of stone breaking. 21 i.e. 12 per cent of them are involved in small stone breaking, 18 i.e. 11 per cent of them loads the stones (*khadi)* into the trucks. 22 i.e. 13 per cent of them are lorry-drivers, 5 i.e. 8 per cent are machine operators, 6 i.e. 4 per cent are supervisors, 6 i.e.4 per cent are tar-labourers, 2 i.e. 1 per cent of them are contractors; while 1 i.e. 0.6 per cent is cleaner of lorry and 1 respondent who is a female is housewife, while remaining 3 i.e. 2 per cent respondents do other kinds of jobs on stone-quarry.

Occupational Status of Spouses of Respondents

Table 4.31 reflects the occupational status of spouses of respondents. In this table, total has gone up to 203, because many of the spouses are involved in two types of jobs e.g. breaking lumps of stones into small pieces and loading the lorries. From the given table it is evident that out of 203, 74 i.e. 36 per cent of the spouses are involved in breaking big lumps of stones into small pieces, 60 i.e. 30 per cent of the spouses are involved in the work of loading trucks, 45 i.e. 22.2 per cent are housewives while 8 i.e. 4 per cent of them are involved in the work of stone breaking. Out of remaining 16, one is tar-labourer and 15 i.e. 17 per cent are involved in other occupations.

Table 4.31

Occupational status of spouses of respondents

Sr. No.	*Occupation*	*Number*	*Percentage*
1.	Big stone breaking	8	4
2.	Small stone breaking	74	36
3.	Loading truck/lorries	60	30
4.	Housewife	45	22.2
5.	Tar labour	1	0.05
6.	Others	15	7
	Total	**203**	**100**

Occupational Status of Wadar Respondents

Table 4.32 shows the occupational status of Wadar respondents. Out of 64, 49 i.e. 76 per cent of the respondents work as 'Tapkari' i.e. stone breaking, 7 i.e. 11 per cent of them are involved in the work of breaking stones into small pieces, 2 i.e. 3 per cent of them loads the lorries with stones, while 3 i.e. 4 per cent of them are drivers. Out of remaining 3 i.e. 6 per cent respondents, one respondent is contractor, one is housewife and remaining one involved in other kind of work of stone quarry.

Table 4.32

Occupational status of Wadar respondents

Sr. No.	*Occupation*	*Number*	*Percentage*
1.	Big stone breaking	49	76
2.	Breaking small stones	7	11
3.	Loading	2	3
4.	Tar labour	0	0
5.	Machine operator	0	0
6.	Contractor	1	2
7.	Supervisor	0	0
8.	Driver	3	4
9.	Cleaner	0	0
10.	Housewife	1	2
11.	Others	1	2
	Total	**64**	**100**

Occupational Status of Spouses of Wadar Respondents

In this section of the chapter an attempt has been made to present the occupational status of the spouses of Wadar respondents.

Table 4.33 (*See on next page)* depicts the occupational status of the spouses of the Wadar respondents. Out of 88, 46 i.e. 52 per cent of the respondent spouses are involved in work of breaking small lumps of stones, 26 i.e. 30 per cent of them do the work of loading the lorries; 1 i.e. 1 per cent respondent breaks the stones and 3 of them i.e. 3 per cent involved in other jobs; while 12 i.e. 14 per cent of them are housewives.

Occupational Status of Laman Respondents (ego)

Table 4.34 reflects that out of 57, 18 i.e. 32 per cent of the Laman respondnets involved in the work of breaking of big stones, 4 i.e. 7 per cent of them involved in small lumps of stones, 8 i.e. 14 per cent of the respondents involved in the work of loading the lorries, 14 i.e. 24 per cent of the respondents are drivers; 6 i.e. 10 per cent of them are tar laboures and 5 i.e. 9 per cent of them are machine operators; while remaining 2 i.e. 4 per cent respondents work as contractor and cleaner respectively.

Table 4.33

Occupational status of spouses of Wadar respondents

Sr. No.	*Occupation*	*Number*	*Percentage*
1.	Big stone breaking	1	1
2.	Small stone breaking	46	52
3.	Loading	26	30
4.	Tar labour	0	0
5.	Cleaner	0	0
6.	Housewife	12	14
7.	Others	3	3
	Total	**88**	**100**

Table 4.34

Occupational status of Laman respondents

Sr. No.	*Occupation*	*Number*	*Percentage*
1.	Big stone breaking	18	32
2.	Breaking small stones	4	7
3.	Loading	8	14
4.	Tar labour	6	10
5.	Machine operator	5	9
6.	Contractor	1	2
7.	Supervisor	0	0
8.	Driver	14	24
9.	Cleaner	1	2
10.	Housewife	0	0
11.	Others	0	0
	Total	**57**	**100**

Occupational status of spouses of Laman respondents

Table 4.35 given below depicts the occupational status of spouses of Laman respondents. Out of 65, 18 i.e. 28 per cent of the spouses of the Laman respondents are housewives, 18 i.e. 28 per cent of the spouses involved in the work of loading the lorries; 14 i.e. 22 per cent of the spouses of respondents are involved in the work of small stone breaking, 12 i.e. 18 per cent of them involved in other work, 2 i.e. 3 per cent of the spouses are involved in the work of big stone breaking; while remaining one spouse of the respondent is tar labourer.

Table 4.35

Occupational status of spouses of Laman respondents

Sr. No.	*Occupation*	*Number*	*Percentage*
1.	Big stone breaking	2	3
2.	Breaking small stones	14	22
3.	Loading	18	28
4.	Tar labourer	1	1
5.	Cleaner	0	0
6.	Housewife	18	28
7.	Others	12	18
	Total	**65**	**100**

Occupational Status of Beldar Respondents

Table 4.36 shows the various types of occupations or jobs of Beldar respondents. Out of 40, 12 i.e. 30 per cent of the respondents are involved in the work of big stone breaking, 9 i.e. 23 per cent of them involved in the work of breaking small stones, 7 i.e. 17 per cent of the respondents involved in the work of loading the lorries; while 6 i.e. 15 per cent of them are supervisors and 5 i.e. 12 per cent of them are drivers.

Occupational Status of Spouses of Beldar Respondents

From the Table 4.37 it is evident that out of 42, 13 i.e. 31 per cent of the spouses of Beldar respondents are housewives; while the number is same for those spouses who are involved in the work of loading the lorries, 11 i.e. 26 per cent of the spouses are involved in the work of breaking small stones and remaining 5 i.e. 12 per cent are involved in the work of big stone breaking.

Table 4.36

Occupational status of Beldar respondents

Sr. No.	*Occupation*	*Number*	*Percentage*
1.	Big stone breaking	12	30%
2.	Breaking small stones	9	23%
3.	Loading	7	17%
4.	Tar labour	0	0
5.	Machine operator	0	0
6.	Contractor	0	0
7.	Supervisor	6	15%
8.	Driver	5	12%
9.	Cleaner	0	0
10.	Housewife	0	0
11.	Others	1	3
	Total	**40**	**100%**

Table 4.37

Occupational status of spouses of Beldar respondents

Sr. No.	*Occupation*	*Number*	*Percentage*
1.	Big stone breaking	5	12
2.	Breaking small stones	11	26
3.	Loading	13	31
4.	Tar labour	0	0
5.	Cleaner	0	0
6.	Housewife	13	31
7.	Others	0	0
	Total	**42**	**100**

Occupational Status of the Tirumal Respondents and their Spouse

Table 4.38 depicts the occupational status of the Tirumal respondents and also their spouses.

Respondent's occupations: It is evident from the table that out of 5 Tirumal respondents, 4 i.e. 80 per cent respondents are involved in the work of big stone breaking; while only one i.e. 20 per cent respondent is in other job.

Spouse's occupations: The table shows that out of 5 spouses, 2 i.e. 40 per cent are housewives and 3 i.e. 60 per cent are involved in the work of breaking small stones.

Table 4.38

Occupational status of Tirumal respondents and their spouses

Sr. No.	*Occupation*	*Respondent*	*Spouse*
		Number	*Number*
1.	Big stone breaking	4	0
2.	Breaking small stones	0	3
3.	Loading stones	0	0
4.	Tar labour	0	0
5.	Machine operator	0	0
6.	Contractor	0	0
7.	Supervisor	0	0
8.	Driver	0	0
9.	Cleaner	0	0
10.	Housewife	0	2
11.	Others	1	0
	Total	**5**	**5**

Annual Income of the Family

Annual income of the family of the respondents is reflected in the Table 4.39. Table shows that maximum number of respondents i.e. 74 (49%) out of 150, have their annual family income between the range of Rs. 40,000 to Rs. 60,000/-, followed by 27 i.e. 18 per cent of respondents who have annual family income between the income range of Rs. 20,000/- to Rs. 40,000/-. 25 i.e. 17 per cent of them are having their annual income between Rs. 60,000/- to Rs. 80,000/-; while 14 i.e. 9 per cent of them have their annual family income within the income range of Rs. 80,000/- to Rs. 1 lakh. Remaining 10 i.e. 7 per cent of the respondents have their annual family income above Rs. one lakh; while only one respondent is having his annual family income up to Rs. 20,000/-.

Table 4.39

Annual income of the family

Sr. No.	*Income range*	*Number*	*Percentage*
1.	Up to Rs. 20,000/-	1	0.6
2.	Rs. 20,000/- to 40,000/-	27	18
3.	Rs. 40,000/- to 60,000/-	74	49
4.	Rs. 60,000/- 80,000/-	25	17
5.	Rs. 80,000/- to 1 lakh	14	9
6.	Above one lakh	10	7
7.	Others	0	0
	Total	**42**	**100**

Annual Family Income of Wadar Respondents

Table 4.40 (*See on next page)* depicts annual family income of Wadar respondents. Maximum of them i.e. 36 means 58 per cent of the respondents have annual family income between the income range of Rs. 40,000/- to 60,000/-, followed by 15 i.e. 24 per cent of them having annual income within the range of Rs. 20,000/- to Rs. 40,000/-; 7 i.e. 11 per cent of respondents have their family income between the income range of Rs. 60,000/- to Rs. 80,000/-; while 2 i.e. 3 per cent of them are having their annual income between the range of Rs. 80,000/- to Rs. one lakh; one i.e. 2 per cent respondent has annual family income above Rs. one lakh; while remaining one respondent's annual family income is up to Rs. 20,000/- only.

Annual Family Income of Laman Respondents

From Table 4.41 it is evident that among Lamans also maximum i.e. 18 (35%), out of 51 respondents have their annual family income within the income range of Rs. 40,000/- to Rs. 60,000/- followed by 13 (25%) respondents who have their annual family income between the range of Rs. 60,000/- to

Rs. 80,000/- 8 i.e. 16% of them have annual family income between Rs. 80,000/- to Rs. one lakh; while 6 i.e. 12 per cent have annual family income above Rs. one lakh; while remaining 6 i.e. 12 per cent have annual family income between Rs. 20,000/- to Rs. 40,000/-.

Table 4.40

Annual family income of Wadar respondents

Sr. No.	*Income range*	*Number*	*Percentage*
1.	Up to Rs. 20,000/-	1	2
2.	Rs. 20,000/- to 40,000/-	15	24
3.	Rs. 40,000/- to 60,000/-	36	58
4.	Rs. 60,000/- 80,000/-	7	11
5.	Rs. 80,000/- to 1 lakh	2	3
6.	Above one lakh	1	3
	Total	**62**	**100**

Table 4.41

Annual Family Income of Laman Respondents

Sr. No.	*Income range*	*Number*	*Percentage*
1.	Up to Rs. 20,000/-	0	0
2.	Rs. 20,000/- to 40,000/-	6	12
3.	Rs. 40,000/- to 60,000/-	18	35
4.	Rs. 60,000/- 80,000/-	13	25
5.	Rs. 80,000/- to 1 lakh	8	16
6.	Above one lakh	6	12
	Total	**51**	**100**

Annual Income of Beldar Respondents

Table 4.42 reflects that, out of 32 respondents, 16 i.e. 50 per cent of the respondents have annual family income between Rs. 40,000/- to Rs. 60,000/-, 5 i.e. 16 per cent of them have annual family income between Rs. 20,000/- to 40,000/- and 5 i.e. 16 per cent have annual income between Rs. 60,000/- to 80,000/-; 3 i.e. 9 per cent of them have their annual family income between

Rs. 80,000/- to Rs. one lakh; while remaining 3 i.e. 9 per cent have their annual family income above Rs. one lakh.

Table 4.42

Annual family income of Beldar respondents

Sr. No.	Income range	Number	Percentage
1.	Up to Rs. 20,000/-	0	0
2.	Rs. 20,000/- to 40,000/-	5	16
3.	Rs. 40,000/- to 60,000/-	16	50
4.	Rs. 60,000/- 80,000/-	5	16
5.	Rs. 80,000/- to 1 lakh	3	9
6.	Above one lakh	3	9
	Total	**32**	**100**

Annual Family Income of Tirumal Respondents

Table 4.43 reflects that out of 5 Tirumal respondents, 2 respondents have their annual family income within the range of Rs. 20,000/- to Rs. 40,000/-, 2 of them have annual family income within the range of Rs. 40,000/- to 60,000/-; while only one respondent have his annual family income between Rs. 60,000/- to 80,000/-.

Table 4.43

Annual family income of Tirumal respondents

Sr. No.	Income range	Number	Percentage
1.	Up to Rs. 20,000/-	0	0
2.	Rs. 20,000/- to 40,000/-	2	40
3.	Rs. 40,000/- to 60,000/-	2	40
4.	Rs. 60,000/- 80,000/-	1	20
5.	Rs. 80,000/- to 1 lakh	0	0
6.	Above one lakh	0	0
	Total	**5**	**100**

Although it is seen from Table 4.39 to 4.43 that the percentage of annual family income among the four communities studied lies between the amount of Rs. 20,000/- to Rs. 60,000/-, the degree of poverty and social insecurity is still high because of the high expenditure incurred on food, health, alcohol, tobacco, gutka, smoking, gambling and other habits.

Earning Members

Table 4.44 given below depicts number of earning members in the 150 families. According to Table 4.44 it is seen that 85 i.e. 57 per cent of the families, out of 150, have two earning members and 42 i.e. 28 per cent families are with one earning member. 17 i.e. 11 per cent families are with three earning members and remaining 6 i.e. 4% families are with four earning members.

Table 4.44

Number of earning members

Sr. No.	*No. of earning members*	*Number*	*Percentage*
1.	One	42	28%
2.	Two	85	57%
3.	Three	17	11%
4.	Four	6	4%
5.	More than four	0	0
	Total	**150**	**100%**

The percentage of having two earning members is as high as 57 per cent.

Earning Members in Wadar Families

From Table 4.45 (*See on next page*) it is evident that out of 62 Wadar families, 42 i.e. 68 per cent families are with two earning members; 12 i.e. 19 per cent of the families are with one earning member, 6 families with three earning members and 2 families with four earning members.

Among the Wadars too, the percentage of two earning members is as high as 68 per cent.

Table 4.45

Number of earning members in Wadar families

Sr. No.	*No. of earning members*	*Number*	*Percentage*
1.	One	12	19
2.	Two	42	68
3.	Three	6	10
4.	Four	2	3
5.	More than four	0	0
	Total	**62**	**100**

Earning Members in Laman Families

Table 4.46 depicts that out of 51 Laman families, 27 i.e. 53 per cent of the families are with two earning members, 16 i.e. 31 per cent families with one earning member, 7 i.e. 14 per cent families are with three earning members and only one i.e. 2 per cent family with four earning members.

Table 4.46

Number of earning members in Laman families

Sr. No.	*No. of earning members*	*Number*	*Percentage*
1.	One	16	31%
2.	Two	27	53%
3.	Three	7	14%
4.	Four	1	2%
5.	More than four	0	0
	Total	**51**	**100%**

Lamans too have 53 per cent of two earning members in the family.

Earning Members in Beldar Families

Table 4.47 reflects that out of 32 Beldar families 13 i.e. 41 per cent are with two earning members, 12 i.e. 37 per cent are with one earning member, 4 i.e. 13 per cent families have three earning members; while 3 i.e. 3 per cent families are with four earning members.

Table 4.47

Number of earning members in Beldar family

Sr. No.	*No. of earning members*	*Number*	*Percentage*
1.	One	12	37
2.	Two	13	41
3.	Three	4	13
4.	Four	3	9
5.	More than four	0	0
	Total	**32**	**100**

Beldars shows 41 per cent of two earning members in the family.

Earning Members in Tirumal Families

Table 4.48 shows that out of 5 Tirumal families, 3 families are with 2 earning members; while 2 families are with only one earning member.

Table 4.48

Number of earning members in Tirumal families

Sr. No.	*No. of earning members*	*Number*	*Percentage*
1.	One	2	40
2.	Two	3	60
3.	Three	0	0
4.	Four	0	0
5.	More than four	0	0
	Total	**5**	**100**

Status of Landholding

Table 4.49 depicts status of landholding of the respondents. The table reflects that out of 150 respondents 99 i.e. 66 per cent of the respondents are landless and 51 i.e. 34 per cent are landholders.

Table 4.49

Status of landholding of respondents

Sr. No.	*Status*	*Number*	*Percentage*
1.	Landless	99	66
2.	Land holders	51	34
	Total	**150**	**100**

Type of Land

The Table 4.50 given below shows the type of land of the respondents who have their own land. From the Table 4.49 it is evident that there are total 51 landholders out of 150 respondents. From Table 4.50 it is seen that out of 51 landholders, 38 i.e. 74 per cent of the landholders have non-irrigated land; 9 i.e. 18 per cent of landholders have irrigated type of land; while 4 i.e. 8 per cent of the landholders have both irrigated and non-irrigated type of land.

Table 4.50

Type of land

Sr. No.	*Type*	*Number*	*Percentage*
1.	Irrigated	9	18
2.	Non-irrigated	38	74
3.	Both type of land	4	8
	Total	**51**	**100**

Caste-wise Status of Landholding

Table 4.51 depicts caste wise status of landholding of respondents. Out of 62 Wadar respondents, 59 i.e. 95 per cent of respondents are landless and only 3 i.e. 5 per cent of them have own land. Among Lamans, the situation is contrast, there are 12 i.e. 23 per cent Laman respondents who are landless and 39 i.e. 77 per cent out of 51, are landholders. Out of 32 Beldars, 27 i.e. 84 per cent of them are landless; while 5 i.e. 16 per cent are landholders. Out of 5 Tirumal respondents, only one respondent is landless and 4 respondents are landholders.

Table 4.51

Caste wise status of landholding of respondents

Sr. No.	*Caste*	*Landholding status*				*Total*	
		Landless		*Landholders*			
		No.	*%age*	*No.*	*%age*	*No.*	*%age*
1.	Wadar	59	95	3	5	62	100
2.	Laman	12	23	39	77	51	100
3.	Beldar	27	84	5	16	32	100
4.	Tirumal	1	20	4	80	5	100
	Total	**99**	**66**	**51**	**34**	**150**	**100**

Table 4.51 clearly shows that 95% Wadars are landless, followed by 84 per cent Beldar, 23 per cent of Laman and 20 per cent of Tirumal.

Castewise Type of Land

Table 4.52 reflects caste wise type of land of the respondents. From the given table, it is seen that 3 Wadar, 5 Beldar and 4 Tirumal have non-irrigated type of land, only Lamans have irrigated and non-irrigated type of land. Out of 39 Laman landholders 9 i.e. 23 per cent have irrigated land, 26 i.e. 67 per cent have non-irrigated type of land and 4 i.e. 10 per cent of them possess both types of land.

Table 4.52 reveals that Lamans possess maximum land and are into cultivation, cattle rearing, and dairy development back at home.

Table 4.52

A comparative table showing type of land

Sr. No.	*Caste*	*Type of land*						*Total*	
		Irrigated		*Non-irrigated*		*Both type of land*			
		No.	*Percentage*	*No.*	*Percentage*	*No.*	*Percentage*	*No.*	*Percentage*
1.	Wadar	0	0	3	100		0	3	100
2.	Laman	9	23	26	67	4	10	39	100
3.	Beldar	0	0	5	100	0	0	5	100
4.	Tirumal	0	0	4	100	0	0	4	100
	Total	**9**	**17**	**38**	**74**	**4**	**9**	**51**	**100**

Possession of Livestock

Table 4.53 depicts the status of possession of livestock among the respondents. Out of 150 respondents, 19 i.e. 13 per cent of the respondents possess livestock; while 131 i.e. 87 per cent of the respondents do not possess livestock.

Table 4.53

Possession of Livestock

Sr. No.	*Status of possession*	*Number*	*Percentage*
1.	Possess	19	13%
2.	Do not possess	131	87%
	Total	**51**	**100%**

General figures on the possession of livestock depicts that 87 per cent of the stone quarry workers do not have live stock but the 13 per cent that posses the same, have it back home in their nature place.

Caste-wise Status of Possession of Livestock

Table 4.54 shows caste wise status of possession of livestock. From the table, it is seen that 2 i.e. 3 per cent, out of

62 Wadar respondents possess livestock and 17 i.e. 33 per cent of the Lamans, out of 51, possess livestock. Beldar and Tirumals do not possess any livestock.

Table 4.54

Caste wise status of possession of Livestock

Sr. No.	*Caste*	*Status of possession*				*Total*	
		Possess		*Do not possess*			
		No.	*Percentage*	*No.*	*Percentage*	*No.*	*Percentage*
1.	Wadar	2	3	60	97	62	100
2.	Laman	17	33	34	67	51	100
3.	Beldar	0	0	32	100	32	100
4.	Tirumal	0	0	5	100	5	100
	Total	**19**	**13**	**131**	**87**	**150**	**100**

Borrowing Behaviour of Stone-quarry Workers

A question was asked to stone-quarry workers as from where do they get money or loan in times of crisis? The sources of loan or borrowing money are reflected in Table 4.55. It is observed that some respondents borrow money from more than one source while some of the respondents do not borrow or take loan. Please note that as respondents have given more than one answer, the total number of respondents have gone upto 193, which should have to be 150.

From Table 4.55 it is evident that out of 193, maximum i.e. 84 means 43 per cent of the respondents borrow money from relatives or friends, followed by 78 i.e. 40 per cent respondents who borrow money from money lender; 4 i.e. 2 per cent of them borrow money from other sources; while 2 i.e. 1 per cent of them borrow money from quarry owner; any one respondent borrow money from the bank; while 24 i.e. 12 per cent respondents do not borrow money.

Table 4.55

Borrowing behaviour

Sr. No.	*Source of loan*	*Number*	*Percentage*
1.	Bank	1	0.5
2.	Patpedhi	0	0
3.	NGO	0	0
4.	Moneylender	78	40
5.	Quarry owner	2	1
6.	Friends/relatives	84	43
7.	Others	4	2
8.	Do not borrow	24	12
	Total	**193**	**100**

Tables 4.55 to 4.58 only reveals that the trend of borrowing money on or without interest is high from moneylenders and relatives/friends. This also means the greater the economic insecurity, the greater the risk of getting loans from banks and financial institutions.

Borrowing Behaviour Among Wadar Respondents

Table 4.56 (*See on next page)* depicts borrowing behaviour among Wadar respondents. From the table given below it is evident that out of 84 respondents, maximum of them i.e. 47 means 56 per cent borrow money from friends and relatives, followed by 32 respondents i.e. 38 per cent borrow money from money lenders; while one respondent borrow money or loan from other sources. Remaining 4 i.e. 5 per cent of them do not borrow money.

Borrowing Behaviour Among Laman Respondents

From Table 4.57 it is evident that out of 68, maximum number of respondents i.e. 37 (55%) respondents borrow money from moneylenders followed by 20 (29%) respondents who borrow money from friends or relatives; 3 (4%) of them borrow money from other sources; 1 (2%) respondent borrow money from quarry owner; while remaining 7 i.e. 10 per cent respondents do not borrow money.

Table 4.56

Source of borrowing money of Wadar respondents

Sr. No.	*Source of loan*	*Number*	*Percentage*
1.	Bank	0	0
2.	Patpedhi	0	0
3.	NGO	0	0
4.	Moneylender	32	38
5.	Quarry owner	0	0
6.	Friends/relatives	47	56
7.	Others	1	1
8.	Do not borrow	4	5
	Total	**84**	**100**

Table 4.57

Source of borrowing money of Laman respondents

Sr. No.	**Source of loan**	**Number**	**Percentage**
1.	Bank	0	0
2.	Patpedhi	0	0
3.	NGO	0	0
4.	Moneylender	37	55
5.	Quarry owner	1	2
6.	Friends/relatives	20	29
7.	Others	3	4
8.	Do not borrow	7	10
	Total	**68**	**100**

Borrowing Behaviour Among Beldars

Table 4.58 reflects that out of 35, 15 i.e. 42 per cent respondents borrow money from relatives or friends; 8 i.e. 23 per cent of them borrow from moneylenders, 1 i.e. 3 per cent respondent borrow money from quarry owner and one respondent borrow money from the bank. Remaining 10 i.e. 29 per cent respondents do not borrow money.

Table 4.58

Source of borrowing money of Beldar respondents

Sr. No.	Source of loan	Number	Percentage
1.	Bank	1	4
2.	Patpedhi	0	0
3.	NGO	0	0
4.	Moneylender	8	23
5.	Quarry owner	1	3
6.	Friends/relatives	15	42
7.	Others	0	0
8.	Do not borrow	10	29
	Total	**35**	**100**

Borrowing Behaviour Among Tirumals

From Table No. 4.59 it is seen that out of 5 Tirumal respondents, 2 respondents borrow money from relatives or friends; while 3 respondents do not borrow money.

Table 4.59

Source of borrowing money of Tirlumals

Sr. No.	Source of loan	Number	Percentage
1.	Bank	0	0
2.	Patpedhi	0	0
3.	NGO	0	0
4.	Moneylender	0	0
5.	Quarry owner	0	0
6.	Friends/relatives	2	40
7.	Others	0	0
8.	Do not borrow	3	60
	Total	**5**	**100**

Frequency of Buying Clothes Per Year

Frequency of buying clothes per year by the stone-quarry workers is reflected in Table 4.60. From the table it is evident that 65 i.e. 43.3 per cent respondents, out of 150 respondents, buy clothes once a year; 80 i.e. 53.3 per cent of them buy clothes from family members and also for themselves twice a year; while remaining 5 i.e. 3.3 per cent of them buy clothes thrice a year.

Table 4.60

Frequency of buying clothes per year

Sr. No.	*Frequency*	*Number*	*Percentage*
1.	Once a year	65	43.3
2.	Twice a year	80	53.3
3.	Thrice a year	5	3.3
	Total	**150**	**100**

Caste wise Frequency of Buying Clothes Per Year

Table 4.61 depicts caste-wise frequency of buying clothes of the respondents per year. Out of 62 Wadar respondents, 42 i.e. 68 per cent buy clothes once a year, 19 (31%) of them buy clothes twice a year; while one respondent buy clothes three times in a year.

Out of 51 Laman respondents, 9 i.e. 18 per cent of the respondents buy clothes once a year, 40 i.e. 78 per cent of them buy clothes twice a year and remaining 2 (4%) buy cloths thrice a year.

Among Beldars it is seen that 13 (41%) respondents, out of 32, buy clothes once a year; 18 i.e. 56 per cent of them buy clothes twice a year and one (3%) respondent buy clothes thrice a year.

Out of 5 Tirumal respondents, 3 (60%) respondents buy clothes twice a year, one respondent buy clothes once a year; while one of them buy clothes thrice a year.

Table 4.61

Caste wise frequency of buying clothes per year

Sr. No.	Caste	Frequency per year						Total	
		Once		Twice		Thrice			
		No.	Percentage	No.	Percentage	No.	Percentage	No.	Percentage
1.	Wadar	42	68	19	31	1	1	62	100
2.	Laman	9	18	40	78	2	4	51	100
3.	Beldar	13	41	18	56	1	3	32	100
4.	Tirumal	1	20	3	60	1	20	5	100
	Total	**65**	**43.3**	**80**	**53.3**	**5**	**33**	**150**	**100**

Economic Assets: A Comparative Analysis

Table 4.62 shows the status of possession of economic assets among stone-quarry workers. It is seen that out of 150 respondents, 104 i.e. 69 per cent of them possess one or more than one asset while 46 i.e. 31 per cent of them do not possess any assets.

Table 4.62

Status of possession of economic assets

Sr. No.	Status	Number	Percentage
1.	Possess	104	69
2.	Do not possess	46	31
	Total	**150**	**100**

An analysis of movable economic assets owned by the four communities studied, is presented in Table 4.63. Thirteen most commonly possessed assets were listed. It was observed that maximum stone quarry workers possess radio/tape recorder for entertainment and of course stove for cooking food. Table 4.63 gives details of the same.

Table 4.63

A comparative table showing asset possession

Sr. No.	Asset	Wadar		Laman		Beldar		Tirumal		Total	
		No.	%	No.	%	No.	%	No.	%	No.	%
1.	Fan	0	0	7	78	2	22	0	0	9	100
2.	Radio/tape recorder	7	39	2	11	8	44	1	6	18	100
3.	Television	0	0	7	50	7	50	0	0	14	100
4.	Clock	0	0	5	38	8	62	0	0	13	100
5.	Wrist watch	13	26	21	41	16	31	1	2	51	100
6.	Cupboard	0	0	0	0	0	0	0	0	0	0
7.	Mobile	1	8	4	33	6	50	1	8	12	100
8.	Bed	0	0	3	25	9	75	0	0	12	100
9.	Table/chairs	0	0	0	0	3	100	0	0	3	100
10.	Stove	26	28	38	41	25	27	4	4	93	100
11.	Gas connection	0	0	0	0	1	100	0	0	1	100
12.	Bicycle	0	0	2	67	1	33	0	0	3	100
13.	Mobike	0	0	0	0	4	100	0	0	4	100
14.	Others	0	0	3	75	1	25	0	0	4	100
	Total	**47**		**92**		**91**		**7**		**237**	

Table 4.63 depicts asset-wise and caste-wise status of possession of assets. It is reflected in the Table 4.62 that out of 150 respondents, 104 respondents possess one or more than one asset. Table 4.63 shows asset wise number of respondents who possess that particular asset. Out of 104, 9 respondents possess fans, among them 7 i.e. 78 per cent are Laman and 2 i.e. 22 per cent aer Beldar and Wadar. Wadars and Tirumals do not possess fans. Out of 104, 18 respondents possess radio/tape recorder, out of these 18 respondents, 7 (39%) are Wadars, 2 (11%) are Lamans; 8 (44%) are Beldars and 1 (6%) is Tirumal. 14 out of 104 respondent have televisions, among them 7 (50%) are Lamans and 7 (50%) are Beldars; 13 respondents possess wall clocks, out of them 5 (38%) are Lamans and 8 (62%) are Beldars. 51 (49%) respondents out of 104 possess wristwatch; out of these 51 respondents 13 (26%) are Wadars, 21 (41%) are Lamans, 16 (31%) are Beldars and remaining one is Tirumal respondent. It is seen that out of 104 respondents not a single respondent possesses cupboard. Out of 104 respondents, 12 respondents possess mobile phones, among these one (8%) respondent is Wadar and one (8%) is Tirumal, 4 (33%) are Laman and 6 (50%) are Beldars. 3 (25%) of the Lamans and 9 (75%) Beldars i.e. total 12 respondents have bed in their houses. Only 3 of the Beldars have table and chairs in their houses. Out of 104 respondents 93 (89%) respondents have stove for cooking food. Out of these 93 respondents 26 (28%) are Wadars, 38 (41%) are Lamans, 25 (27%) are Beldars, 4 (4%) are Tirumals.

Out of 104, only one respondent who is Beldar possess cooking gas connection. 2 of the Lamans and one Beldar i.e. total 3 respondents, out of 104, have their own bicycles, while 4 respondents who are Beldar, out of 104, have their own mobikes. Remaining 4 respondents, out of 104, possess other assets.

Ownership of House

Table 4.64 depicts the type of ownership of house of the respondents. From the Table 4.64 it is seen that out of 150 respondents, 147 i.e. 98 per cent of the respondents live in a houses provided by quarry owners. These houses are situated in the area which is nearby the quarry. Remaining 3 i.e. 2 per cent respondents are living in houses on rental basis, two of them are Beldar and one is Wadar respondent.

Table 4.64

Ownership status of house of respondents

Sr. No.	*Status*	*Number*	*Percentage*
1.	Own	0	0
2.	Rental	3	2
3.	Provided by quarry owner	147	98
	Total	**150**	**100**

Type of House

Table 4.65 reflects on types of houses of the respondents. From the table it is evident that out of 150 respondents, 52 (35%) respondents are living in the houses made up of bricks as walls and tin/cement sheets as roof; 38 (25%) of the respondents are living in the tents or huts made up of plastic sheets; 34 (23%) of them are living in the houses with tin sheets walls and tin or cement or plastic sheets as roof; 20 (13%) of the respondents are living in the houses which are made up of stones, where walls are of stones and the roof is of either tin or cement sheets or of plastic sheets; 5 i.e. 3 per cent of the respondent are living in huts made up of palm leaves.

Table 4.65

Types of houses of respondents

Sr. No.	*House Type*	*No.*	*Percentage*
1.	Brick walls – tin/cement sheets roof	52	35
2.	Stick walls – thatched/plastic sheets roof	1	1
3.	Tin walls – tin/cement/plastic/tiled roof	34	23
4.	Stone walls – tin/cement/tiled roof	20	13
5.	Plastic sheets tent	38	25
6.	Palm leaves hut	5	3
	Total	**150**	**100**

House Types of Wadars

It is observed from Table 4.66 that out of 62 Wadar stone workers, maximum of them i.e. 37 (60%) are living in the tent or hut like structure made up of plastic sheets; 14 i.e. 22 per cent of the Wadar respondents are living in the houses made up of tin sheets as walls and roof of tin/cement/plastic sheets; while remaining 5 respondents (8%) are living in the houses made up of stones as walls and roof of either tin sheets or cement sheets or of plastic sheets.

Table 4.66

House types of Wadars

Sr. No.	*House type*	*Number*	*Percentage*
1.	Brick walls – tin/cement sheets roof	6	10
2.	Stick walls – thatched/plastic sheets roof	0	0
3.	Tin walls – tin/cement/plastic/tiled roof	14	22
4.	Stone walls – tin/cement/tiled roof	5	8
5.	Plastic sheets tent	37	60
6.	Palm leaves hut	0	0
	Total	**62**	**100**

House Types of Lamans

Table 4.67 reflects that out of 51 Laman respondents 23 i.e. 45 per cent Laman respondents are living in the houses made up of brick walls and tin/cement sheets' roof; 12 i.e. 23 per cent of them have house with tin walls and tin/cement or plastic sheets' roof; 9 i.e. 18 per cent of them are living in the houses with stone walls and tin/plastic sheets' as roof. Out of remaining 7 respondents, 3 i.e. 6 per cent of them are living in tents/huts made up of plastic sheets; while other 3 i. 6 per cent are living in the houses made up of palm leaves and 1 respondent (2%) is living in a house made up of stick walls and thatched or plastic sheet roof.

Table 4.67

Types of houses of respondents

Sr. No.	*House type*	*No.*	*Percentage*
1.	Brick walls – tin/cement sheets roof	23	45
2.	Stick walls – thatched/plastic sheets roof	1	2
3.	Tin walls – tin/cement/plastic/tiled roof	12	23
4.	Stone walls – tin/cement/tiled roof	9	18
5.	Plastic sheets tent	3	6
6.	Palm leaves hut	3	6
	Total	**51**	**100**

House Type of Beldars

From Table 4.68 it is seen that out of 32 Beldar respondents, 18 i.e. 56 per cent of the Beldars are having the houses of brick walls and tin or cement sheets as roof; 8 i.e. 25 per cent are living in the houses made up of tin sheets' as walls and tin/ cement or plastic sheets' as roof; while remaining 6 i.e. 19 per cent of the Beldar respondents are living in the stone houses.

Table 4.68

House types of Beldars

Sr. No.	*House type*	*No.*	*Percentage*
1.	Brick walls – tin/cement sheets roof	18	56
2.	Stick walls – thatched/plastic sheets roof	0	0
3.	Tin walls – tin/cement/plastic/tiled roof	8	25
4.	Stone walls – tin/cement/tiled roof	6	19
5.	Plastic sheets tent	0	0
6.	Palm leaves hut	0	0
	Total	**32**	**100**

House Types of Tirumal

It is observed during the fieldwork that all the 5 Tirumal respondents are living in the houses, which are made up of stones as walls and tin or cement sheets as roof.

Tables 4.64 to 4.68 reveal an interesting finding that maximum number of stone quarry workers are given houses to live in by the quarry owners. However, the labourers have no other choice, but to live in any type of house provided by the owner. Table 4.69 reveals that 93 per cent of the families studied live in house having an area of less than 200 sq. feet.

Area of House

From Table 4.69 it is seen that the maximum number of respondents i.e. 140 (93%) respondents, out of 150, have the area of their houses less than 200 sq. feet; 9 i.e. 6 per cent of the respondents have the area of house from 200 sq. feet to 350 sq. feet; while only one respondent's house is of area between 350 sq. feet to 500 sq. feet.

Table 4.69

Area of house

Sr. No.	*Area in sq. feet*	*Number*	*Percentage*
1.	Less than 200 sq.ft.	140	93
2.	200 sq.ft. to 350 fq.ft.	9	6
3.	350 sq.ft. to 500 sq. ft.	1	1
4.	Above 500 sq. ft.	0	0
	Total	**150**	**100**

Status of Ventilation of the House

From Table 4.70 it is seen that out of 150 houses, only 15 i.e. 10 per cent houses have adequate ventilation; while 135 i.e. 90 per cent of the houses are without adequate ventilation.

Table 4.70

Status of ventilation of houses of respondents

Sr. No.	*Status of ventilation*	*Number*	*Percentage*
1.	Adequate ventilation	15	10
2.	Inadequate ventilation	135	90
	Total	**150**	**100**

CHILDREN OF STONE QUARRY WORKERS

The researcher has covered 150 respondents i.e. 150 families. Total population of 150 families is 620, out of which 336 are adults and 284 are children (up to 18 years). Out of 336 adults, 177 (53%) are males and 159 (47%) are females. Among the children 152 (53.5%) are male children and 132 (46.5%) are female children.

Age-range of Children of Respondents

Age and sex wise break-up of the children has been given in following Table 4.71. Here, children are divided according to the age range.

Table 4.71

Age and sex wise break-up of children of respondents

Sr. No.	*Age range*	*Sex*				*Total*	
		Male		*Female*			
		No.	*Percent-age*	*No.*	*Percent-age*	*No.*	*Percent-age*
1.	Up to 1 yr.	12	41	17	59	29	100
2.	1 yr. to 6 yr.	64	56	51	44	115	100
3.	6 yr. to 14 yrs.	56	50	56	50	112	100
4.	14 yrs. to 18 yrs.	20	71	8	29	28	100
	Total	**152**		**132**		**284**	

Educational Status of Children

Table 4.72 depicts the education status of children of 150 respondents.

Out of 284 children, 119 (42%) of the children go to school and 165 (58%) of the children do not go to school.

Out of 119 school-going children 68 i.e. 57 per cent are males and 51 i.e. 43 per cent are females. Out of 165 non-school going children 86 (52%) are males and 79 (48%) are females.

Table 4.72

School going and non-school going children

Sr. No.	*Status of schooling*	*Sex*				*Total*	
		Male		*Female*			
		No.	*Percent-age*	*No.*	*Percent-age*	*No.*	*Percen-age*
1.	School going	68	57	51	43	119	100
2.	Non-school going	86	52	79	48	165	100
	Total	**154**	**54**	**130**	**46**	**284**	**100**

An N.G.O. by the name 'Santulan' is working in the field of education of the stone quarry workers. "Pashan Shala Project" i.e. schools for the stone quarry workers has been established with Government funding and hence school going children's percentage is good.

Wadar Children

Table 4.73 depicts age and sex wise division of children of Wadar respondents. Out of total 284 children, 119 i.e. 42 per cent are Wadar children. Out of 119 Wadar children 68 i.e. 57 per cent are males and 51 i.e. 43 per cent are females. From the Table 4.72 it is evident that, out of total 119 Wadar children 15 children are infants i.e. they are up to one year of age. Out of 15 infants, 7 (47%) are males and 8 (53%) are females. 48 of the Wadar children are within the age range of 1 to 6 years. Out of these 48 children 27 (56%) are males and 21 (44%) are females.

The number of children within the age range of 6 to 13 years is 44, out of total 119 children. Out of 44 children 24 (55%) are males and 20 (45%) are females. Remaining 12 children out of 119 children are within the age range of 13 years to 18 years. Out of 12 children 10 (83%) are males and 2 (12%) are females.

Table 4.73

Age range of Wadar children

Sr. No.	*Age*	*Sex*				*Total*	
		Male		*Female*			
		No.	*Percent-age*	*No.*	*Percent-age*	*No.*	*Percent-age*
1.	0 to 1 yr.	7	47	8	53	15	100
2.	1 yr. to 6 yrs.	27	56	21	44	48	100
3.	6 yrs. to 13 yrs.	24	55	20	45	44	100
4.	13 yrs. to 18 yrs.	10	83	2	17	12	100
	Total	**68**	**57**	**51**	**43**	**119**	**100**

Schooling Status of Wadar Children

Table 4.74 reflects on status of schooling of the Wadar children. Out of 119 Wadar children, 39 (33%) children go to school and 80 (67%) of the children do not go to school.

Out of 39 school-going children 23 (59%) are males and 16 (41%) are females; while out of 80 non-school going children 45 (56%) are males and 35 (44%) are females.

Laman Children

Table 4.75 provides age and sex-wise division of children of Laman respondents. Out of total 284 children, 90 (32%) children are Lamans, and out of 90 Laman children 49 i.e. 54 per cent are males; while 41 i.e. 46 per cent are females.

Table 4.74

Status of school going Wadar children

Sr. No.	Status of schooling	Sex				Total	
		Male		Female			
		No.	Percent-age	No.	Percent-age	No.	Percent-age
1.	School going	23	59	16	41	39	100
2.	Non-school going	45	56	35	44	80	100
	Total	**68**	**57**	**51**	**43**	**119**	**100**

According to the table given below, it is seen that out of 90 Laman children, 6 are upto one year old, out of which 3 are males and 3 are females. Children between the age-range of 1 to 6 years are 42, out of these 24 i.e. 57 per cent are males and 18 i.e. 43 per cent are females. The number of children within the age-range of 6 years to 13 years is 29, out of these 29 children, 14 (48%) are males and 15 (52%) are females. Remaining 13 children are within the age-range of 13 to 18 years, out of them 8 are males and 5 are females.

Table 4.75

Age range of Laman children

Sr. No.	Age-range	Sex				Total	
		Male		Female			
		No.	Percent-age	No.	Percent-age	No.	Percent-age
1.	Up to 1 yr.	3	50	3	50	6	100
2.	1 yr. to 5 yrs.	24	57	18	43	42	100
3.	5 yrs. to 13 yrs.	14	48	15	52	29	100
4.	13 yrs. to 18 yrs.	8	62	5	38	12	100
	Total	**49**	**54**	**41**	**46**	**90**	**100**

Schooling Status of Laman Children

Table 4.76 depicts that out of 90 Laman children 35 (39%) children attend school and 55 (61%) of the children do not attend school. Out of 35 school-going children 23 (66%) are males and 12 (34%) are females. Out of 55 non-school going children 27 (49%) are males and 28 (51%) are females.

Table 4.76

Schooling status of Laman children

Sr. No.	*Status*	*Sex*				*Total*	
		Male		*Female*			
		No.	*Percent-age*	*No.*	*Percent-age*	*No.*	*Percent-age*
1.	School going	23	66	12	34	35	100
2.	Non school going	27	49	28	51	55	100
	Total	**50**	**56**	**40**	**44**	**90**	**100**

Beldar Children

From the Table 4.77 (*See on next page*) it is evident that out of 284 children, 64 (23%) are Beldar children, among them 30 (47%) are males land 34 (53%) are females.

The table also depicts that out of 64 Beldar children, 7 are up to the age of one year, out of them one is male and 6 are females. 19 children, out of 64, are within the age range of 1 to 6 years, out of them 11 i.e. 58 per cent are males land 8 i.e. 42 per cent are females. The number of children within the age range of 6 to 13 years, is 35, out of them 16 i.e. 46 per cent are males and 19 i.e. 54 per cent are females. Remaining 3 children are within the age range of 13 to 18 years. Out of them two are males and one is female.

Schooling Status of Beldar Children

It is evident from Table 4.78 that out of 64 Beldar children 40 (62.5%) children attend school; while 24 (37.5%) do not attend school. Out of 40 school-going children 20 (50%) are males and

20 (50%) are females; while out of 24 non-school going children 11 (46%) are males and 13 (54%) are females.

Table 4.77

Age range of Beldar children

Sr. No.	Age	Sex				Total	
		Male		Female			
		No.	Percent-age	No.	Percent-age	No.	Percent-age
1.	0 to 1 yr.	1	14	6	86	7	100
2.	1 yr. to 6 yrs.	11	58	8	42	19	100
3.	6 yrs. to 13 yrs.	16	46	19	54	35	100
4.	13 yrs. to 18 yrs.	2	67	1	33	3	100
	Total	**30**	**47**	**34**	**53**	**64**	**100**

Table 4.78

School and non-school going Beldar children

Sr. No.	Status	Sex				Total	
		Male		Female			
		No.	Percent-age	No.	Percent-age	No.	Percent-age
1.	School going	20	50	20	50	40	100
2.	Non school going	11	46	13	54	24	100
	Total	**31**	**48**	**33**	**52**	**64**	**100**

Tirumal Children

From Table 4.79 it is revealed that, out of 284 children, 11 children are Tirumals, among them 5 (45%) are males and 6 (55%) are females. Out of 11 Tirumal children only one male child is up to one year of age; 6 of them are within the age range of 1 to 6 years, among these 6 children, 2 are males and 4 are females. Remaining 4 children are within the age range of 6 to 13 years. Out of these 4 children, 2 are males and 2 are females.

Table 4.79

Age range of Tirlumal children

Sr. No.	*Age range*	*Male*	*Females*	*Total*
		Number	*Number*	
1.	Up to 1 yr.	1	0	1
2.	1 yr. to 5 yrs.	2	4	6
3.	5 yrs. To 13 yrs.	2	2	4
4.	13 yrs. to 18 yrs.	0	0	0
	Total	**5**	**6**	**11**

Schooling Status of Tirumal Children

From Table 4.80 it is evident that, out of 11 Tirumal children, 5 (45%) are school going children; while 6 (55%) children do not go to school. Out of 5 school-going children 2 are males land 3 are females; while out of 6 non-school going children 3 are males and 3 are females.

Table 4.80

Schooling status of Tirumal children

Sr. No.	*Status*	*Male*	*Females*	*Total*
		Number	*Number*	
1.	School going	2	3	5
2.	Mpm-school going	3	3	6
	Total	**5**	**6**	**11**

DISCUSSIONS

It is evident from the primary data presented in Chapter Four on the socio-economic status of all the four communities, that each of the caste group which was traditionally into stone work/business have taken up the same profession despite of the technological advances. With the introduction of new technology such as stone-crushing machines, drilling gadgets, blasting techniques and introduction of trucks etc. the young generation of Wadars, Lamans, Beldars and Tirumals are opting for job, such as drivers, crushing machine operators, drill machine operators, tar and stone mixer operators etc. These changes are certainly taking place among these communities. In fact, some of these groups who have settled in slums are working as contractors and dealers in the construction industry.

A comparative analysis of few indicators has been presented in this section of the Chapter. These are as follows:

- **Settlement Pattern and House Types**

Out of all the four communities it was observed that the Wadars lived in plastic sheets' tents and tin houses. Out of the total sample of 150 respondents 62 were Wadar respondents. Out of these 62 Wadars, 37 i.e. 60 per cent live in temporary tents made up of plastic sheets; while remaining 14 i.e. 22 per cent live in tin houses and 5 i.e. 8 per cent live houses made up of stone walls and tin roofs; while only 6 i.e. 10 per cent live in houses made up of brick walls and tin or cement sheets roof. Details about settlement pattern and house types of Lamans, Beldars and Tirumals are given in this chapter. The reason why the Wadars live in plastic tents and temporary houses is because of the characteristic nomadism, landlessness and poverty.

- **Educational Status**

Illiteracy rate among the total sample was found to be very high. It was observed that out of 150 respondents, 102 i.e. 68 per cent were illiterate. It was also shocking to note that out of 150 respondents, 133 were males. 115 spouses (females) of the 133 male respondents were illiterate. Furthermore, caste-wise statistics reveal that out of 62 Wadar respondents 48 (i.e. 77%) were illiterate. Similarly, out of the total 51 Laman respondents 34 i.e.67 per cent were illiterates. Out of total 32 Beldars 18 i.e. 56.3 per cent were illiterates. Yet another interesting finding regarding illiteracy status of the spouses of the target population is concerned the facts are as follows. It was observed that 58 i.e. 100 per cent of Wadar, 38 i.e. 74 per cent of Laman, 16 i.e. 50 per cent of Beldars and 3 i.e. 60 per cent of Tirumals were illiterate.

- **Social Status**

Despite of the rapid urbanisation, modernisation and technologcal advancement the social position of the Wadars, Lamans, Beldars and Tirumals in the caste hierarchy as viewed by them as well as other caste groups remains the same. They are still branded a caste communities associated with stone, construction and transportation work. Constitutionally all these communities have been listed in the nomadic communities of Maharashtra's schedule list. This social status was and is part of their social life despite of the social changes and occupational shifts that have come into these communities. Their settlement patterns and community solidarity at the quarries are distinct features of their social status, even at the quarries, which are so close to the urban areas and influenced by the urbanisation. Every caste group lives together in separate settlements in a commonly occupied in a quarry or land. Although it is seen that on common big patch of land there are several stone quarry owners having all these three communities, still one gets to see even stone quarry owners who work very closely to each other have these communities staying separately in separate settlement even on a separate patch of land. This proves that caste component is directly influencing community solidarity among the stone quarry workers. Rituals related to festivities and life transitions are observed by these communities among themselves. This proves that caste factor promotes and strengthens strong community bonds. As regards interaction with each other there are some aspects, where interaction within these groups takes place especially while drinking liquor, gambling, going to the markets etc. Whereas inter-caste marriages are prohibited.

- **Economic Status**

(i) Annual Income

Out of 150 respondents studied 74 i.e. 49 per cent of the respondents' income ranges from Rs. 40,000/- to Rs. 60,000/-. This income range is certainly above the Government of India's BPL (Below Poverty Line) norms. This is because, both the spouses along with teenaged, youth or married children in case of joint family earn. Hence the family's annual income range is above Rs. 20,000/- per annum.

A comparative analysis of the family's income among the four groups it is seen that income range above Rs. 80,000/- is seen among 28 per cent of Lamans, 18 per cent of Beldars and only 5 per cent of Wadars and none among the Tirumals. Here again the Wadar show less income level as compared to the other groups.

(ii) Landless and Landholders

Out of 150 respondents studied 66 per cent were landless and 34 per cent were landholders. A comparative analysis of the four groups studied reveals that maximum landless respondents were among Wadars 95 per cent followed by Beldars, 84 per cent.

Caste-wise comparison of landholders highlights that Tirumals were maximum landholders followed by Lamans.

The Lamans who are basically from Rajasthan have migrated to sourthern parts of India, in Karnataka, Andhra and South of Maharashtra, worked for the Nizams once upon a time may have been given land by the Muslim Kings. Secondly, since they have settled in these areas for over 200 to 300 years may be having their forefather's land and house, hence they are different from the other communities. The study also revealed that Lamans have maximum irrigated land; while the Wadars and Beldars possess non-irrigated and waste land.

(iii) Possession of Livestock

Out of 150 respondents interviewed, 19 i.e. 13 per cent respondents possess livestock. A comparative analysis of the four caste groups revealed that out of 19, 17 i.e. 90 per cent are Lamans and 2 i.e. 10 per cent are Wadars, while none of the Beldar and Tirumal possess livestock.

As mentioned earlier that maximum Lamans possess agriculture land, hence it is but natural that this group also possess livestock.

(iv) Economic Assets

An attempt was done to find out economic assets possessed by the target population. These assets were fan, radio/tape recorder, television, clock, wrist watch, cupboard, mobile, bed, table, chairs, stove, cooking gas connection, bicycle, mobike and other items including mixer, utensils, baskets etc. The immovable assets like land and house, which are prominently found among the Lamans. Out of the movable assets radio/taperrecorders and stoves were found among all the 4 groups. It is also observed that due to mobility and nomadic nature among all the four communities, the degree of possession of movable assets is very less.

(v) Job Status

It was observed that all 150 families working for the stone quarry owners do not have permanent job or any job security. Some of them move within the quarry to work for other quarry owners in case of job crisis.

(vi) Skilled and Unskilled Work

Considering the socio-economic status of Wadars, it may be said that the degree of unskilled manpower and labour high. While the percentage of skilled manpower/labour such as stone crusher operators, drivers, drill machine operators, supervisors etc. is high among the Laman and Beldars as their socio-economic status is higher than the Wadars.

(vii) Number of Earning Members

Since all the respondents studied are daily wage labourers and that there is no job security, both the spouses work, so as to get sufficient income for the family. It was observed that the numbers of earning members among Wadars are more followed by Lamans, Beldars and Tirumals.

(viii) Weekly Payment

Greater the economic need and urgency of cash, earlier the payment. All respondents are basically hand to mouth, and are also addicted to alcohol, smoking, chewing tobacco and gutka, gambling hence tend to spend cash faster. In such cases payments are made weekly. This only points out the insecure and temporary job status of respondents.

(ix) Borrowing Behaviour

It was observed that the percentage of borrowing money in times of crisis from friends and relatives and by moneylenders is very high among stone-quarry workers. Facts revealed in Chapter Four about the socio-economic status of the stone quarry workers in general, as well as individual caste groups, reveals that low social, economic, educational, health, nutritional and political profile of the stone quarry workers have made them victims of social insecurity. The quarry owners do provide some with housing security, which is temporary, is not good enough to secure them.

5

HEALTH, NUTRITION AND ENVIRONMENTAL ISSUES OF STONE QUARRY WORKERS

HEALTH POLICY: AN INTRODUCTION

India was committed to achieving "Health Policy" approved by the Parliament in 1983, accepted primary health care as the main instrument to achieving Health for All (HFA) by 2000 A.D. In order to ensure H.F.A., both State and Central Governments have established a vast network of rural and urban health institutions in the country. The purpose of these institutions was to provide comprehensive health services to the people.

Efforts are being made to ensure that the health services provided by the rural and urban health infrastructure are:

- Accessible to the people
- Available on continuing basis
- Acceptable culturally and socially
- Affordable by most of the people

During the decade of 1980-90 a vast network of rural institutions like Sub-Centres (SCs), Primary Health Centres (PHC) and Community Health Centres (CHC) were established.

Unfortunately, these health centres have not been able to provide the people with good quality health care.

Instead of providing comprehensive "health care" they have emphasised on "medical care". Promotive and preventive health services have not received the emphasis and attention they deserve. While rural health services are being developed on a relatively normative pattern. It is disheartening to note that in spite of the fact that the urban population of India, by the turn of the century has become about one third of the total Indian population, no serious effort is being made systematically to develop an urban Health Service Network. For instance the rapidly growing slum and pavement population have no proper health services. This has created several health and nutritional problems to the Indian people. (Tribhuwan Robin, 2004).

National Health Policy

It was in this context that the National Health Policy (NHP) was evolved. In 1983, the country adopted the National Policy. The primary objective of the NHP was to attain the goal of Health for For All by 2000 A.D. by establishing an effective and efficient health care system for all citizens, especially vulnerable groups like women, children and the under privileged.

The National Health Policy strongly stressed, the creation of an infrastructure for primary health care in the country. Other major priority areas are close co-ordination with health related services and activities (like nutrition, drinking water supply and sanitation), the active involvement and participation of voluntary organisation; the provision of essential drugs and vaccines, qualitative improvement in health and family planning services, the provision of adequate training; and medical research aimed at the common health problems of the people (GOI 1983).

Critique of the NHP

Any review of the National Health Policy must take into account three questions:

- Does the National Health Policy reflect the ground realities in the provision of health care sufficiently?
- Have the goals of the National Health Policy been fulfilled?

- Were these goals and the action taken adequate to meeting the basic goal of the National Health Policy of providing 'universal' comprehensive primary health care services, relevant to the actual needs and priorities of the community?

In the decade following 1980, rural health care received special attention. Massive infrastructure expansion and programmes for providing primary health care facilities were undertaken in the sixth and seventh Five Year Plans to achieve the target of one Primary Health Centre (PHC) for 30,000 people and on the Sub Centre (SC) per 5,000 people in the plains, and one PHC for 20,000 people and one SC for 3,000 people in tribal and hilly areas. (Tribhuwan Robin, 2004).

Health Care and Health Infrastructure for Unorganised Sectors, People and Settlements

The national health policy no doubt advocated health care and infrastructure for the rural areas through its vast network of PHCs, Sub-Centres and ICDS Units. Similarly, in the urban areas health care and infrastructure was provided through municipal corporations, hospitals as well as government hospitals such as Sasoon Hospital in Pune, G.T. and J.J. Hospital in Mumbai and Ghati Hospital in Aurangabad. This effort to achieve health for all by the year 2000 A.D. was not enough. Number of settlements and habitation of people belonging to the unorganised sectors such as brick kilns, sugarcane workers, nomads, construction workers, stone quarry workers, pavement dwellers etc. still do not have a separate infrastructure and manpower to impart health and nutrition services to them. This chapter focusses on the health care, nutritional and environmental issues of the stone quarry workers.

HEALTH ISSUES OF STONE QUARRY WORKERS

Stone quarry workers from an unorganized sector of industry scattered all over India. There are various procedures and operations involved in this work viz. blasting, drilling, stone-cutting, stone-breaking, loading, crushing, transporting. Based on these operations, the workers are employed at different places as per the nature of work and are exposed to silica dust of different concentration. (Ghotkar, Maldhure, Zodpey, 1995).

The mining and quarrying sector is traditionally a sector that posses large risks to occupational health and safety. The most important occupational risks related to stone quarrying include:

- fatal accidents
- physical injuries requiring medical treatments
- work related illnesses : respiratory diseases such as silicosis and tuberculosis due to inhalation of dust.

Work related illnesses endemic to the stone industry include the respiratory diseases silicosis and tuberculosis due to prolonged inhalation of silica-dust (from quartz particles) (www.hinduon net.com). Silicosis is particularly relevant to the siliceous natural stone industry. (Granite, sandstone). Dangerous levels and respirable quartz particles (exceeding 0.1 mg/m^3) have been reported in many industries world-wide and are most frequently found in, amongst others, granite quarrying and processing as well as in crushed stone and related industries (IARC, 1997).

Health and safety issues in stone processing facilities include dust and noise in the cutting process and the manual carrying quarrying of heavy weights. (CREM, 2006).

A report on public health in Gujarat revealed that the number of people suffering from tuberculosis (TB) and silicosis is rising rapidly. Silicosis is an occupational lung disease caused by the inhalation of silica particles, mostly from quartzes in rocks and sand. Tuberculosis is a transmittable disease that is easily communicated among workers in industries with high dust emissions. The incidence of these two fatal diseases among workers in stone cutting factories and quarries is relatively high. To certain extent, these diseases may be prevented by wetting the rocks before processing and by using modern machinery to minimise dust generation (Hindustan Times, 2005). But wet cutting hardly appears to be the norm, in particular in manual processing. In mechanised plants, wet cutting is applied in the cutting and polishing process for two reasons. Water is not only used to prevent high dust emissions (Sengupta, 2005), but also to cool the saw blades that might otherwise be damaged because of the extreme heat generated during cutting process.

A study conducted at stone quarries situated in east of Nagpur by Ghotkar V.B., Maldhure B.R. and Zodpey S.P. has found 32.5 per cent prevalence of respiratory morbidity in stone quarry workers, on the basis of radiological appearance.

Another not common occupational hazard in quarrying involves hearing impairment due to long term exposure to noise. Noise levels are often very high, ranging between 58 to 88 db from processes such as blasting. Continued exposure to such noise levels can cause serious hearing problems. (CREM, 2006).

The machines used for stone cutting and polishing in mechanised plants can generate noise levels of 75 to 85 dB in the working area. Continued exposure to this level of noise is very harmful. The Stone Track Corporation was found to provide earmuffs for its workers, but many workers fail to wear these. Likely, their supervisors do not oblige them to do so and the workers are insufficiently aware of the hazards, lack the necessary training and are simply not used to wearing protective equipment(Sengupta, 2005).

Workers are also required to carry very heavy weights, mainly in shallow quarries and non-mechanised plants. Basic safety provisions, such as dust masks, protective shoes, gloves are largely absent (CREM, 2006).

Most processing plants use cranes to unload raw materials from their trucks and reload them with their finished products. Tiles or slabs are usually packed in large boxes that are so heavy that they cannot be carried manually. However, it is common practice for heavy blocks or slabs to be manually carried from the loading platforms to the processing site (Sengupta, 2005).

Accidents at work, sometimes resulting in the death of workers, occur frequently in quarries. This study has revealed that the unsecured and poor stone quarry workers become constant victims of small and serious accidents. In fact there are several case studies of stone quarry workers resulting into deaths during rock blast, land slides and truck accidents. Given below are few case studies revealing the above facts.

Case Studies of Accidents and Injuries

Although statistical data presented in this chapter reveals problems related to health and nutrition of stone quarry workers and their children, few case studies related to health and nutritional insecurities have been reported in this and chapter No. 6. In this section of the chapter, brief case studies have been presented to highlight why injuries and accidents take place at the quarries. The chapter on review of literature also highlights case studies on health insecurity of stone quarry workers in south Gujarat carried out by a German Sociologist by the name Jan Breman in his book captioned "Footloose Labour".

Case Studies

Sr. No.	*Name and background*	*Course of events and Analysis*
I.	Nura Rathod, aged 32, a male member of Laman community and driver by profession has been working in Moshi stone quarry for last 12 years. Prior to becoming driver he worked as a labourer.	He narrated his experience of how he was hurt on his chin while loading stones in the truck. One of the sharp stones fell on his chin and tore it to certain extent. It was bleeding heavily. He himself went to the hospital. His chin had to be stitched by the doctors. He had five stitches on the same. Although his owner paid him the entire medical expenses of Rs. 4000/-, Nura has those deep marks of stitches on his chin. Nura said, "These marks on our bodies remind us about our profession". Several workers like Nura become victims of such
II.	Sangita Chavan, aged 30, a female member of Beldar caste is working at Moshi stone quarry site. She works as daily wage labourer for loading trucks, breaking lumps of stones into small pieces, carrying	

(Contd...)

Sr. No.	Name and background	Course of events and Analysis
II.	stones from one place to other. Since last ten years she is living in Moshi near stone quarry site with her family.	accidents but continue to work at the quarries because of illiteracy, poverty, and lack of professional skills. Sangita Chavan told about her experience of how she is suffering from major health problem caused due to heavy work at stone quarry. Initially, she had pain in her back-bone, but she ignored that. One day while carrying a big stone, she experienced severe pain in her vertebral column and she was not able to work. Doctor told her that there is gap in her back-bone and that she should not do heavy work. She spent about Rs. 3500/- for her treatment. Quarry owner did not give her a single rupee for treatment though she is suffering from spondylitis. She has to work for survival. Like Sangita there are several stone quarry workers both men and women, suffering from major or minor health problems, but cannot take treatment due to lack of sufficient financial support.

Place of Treatment

Table 5.1 shows the place of treatment of respondents. From the table it is evident that maximum number of respondents prefers to go to private clinic or hospital. Out of 200, 148 i.e. 74 per cent respondents go to private doctor for treatment and according to Table 5.2, (*See on page 170*) out of 148, 62 i.e. 42 per cent are Wadars, 50 i.e. 34 per cent are Lamans, 31 i.e. 21 per cent are Beldars and 5 i.e. 3 per cent Tirumals. Out of 200, 50 respondents prefer to go at Government Hosptials and according to Table No. 5.2, out of 50, 8 i.e. 16 per cent are Wadars, 19 i.e. 38 per cent are Lamans, 20 i.e. 40 per cent are Beldars and 3 i.e. 6 per cent are Beldars. Remaining two respondents go to municipal hospitals.

Tabel 5.1

Place of medical treatment

Sr. No.	*Place of treatment*	*Number*	*Percentage*
1.	PHC	0	0
2.	Sub Centre	0	0
3.	Rural Hospital	0	0
4.	Private doctor/clinic	148	74
5.	Municipal Hospital	2	1
6.	Government Hospital	50	25
7.	Traditional Medical Practitioner	0	0
8.	Any other place	0	0
	Total	**200**	**100**

Place of Deliveries of Women Stone Quarry Workers

Table 5.3 shows (*See on page 171*) the places of deliveries conducted of the women stone quarry workers. From the table it is evident that, out of 154, maximum i.e. 125 i.e. 81 per cent of the women delivered at home. Out of these 125 women, 55 i.e. 44 per cent are Wadar women, 38 i.e. 30 per cent are Laman women, 27 i.e. 22 per cent are Beldar and 5 i.e. 4 per cent are Tirumal women.

Out of 154, 6 (4%) women delivered at private hospital. Out of these 6, 4 women are Wadar and 2 women are Beldar. 8 women i.e. 5 per cent, out of 154 delivered at Municipal Hospitals. Out of these 8, 3 are Wadar women, 3 Beldar women and 2 Laman women. Out of 154, 5 i.e. 3 per cent women delivered at Government Hospital, all these 5 women are Beldar women.

Personnel Conducting Deliveries

Table 5.4 (*See on page 172*) reflects on the personnel who conducted the deliveries of stone quarry worker women. It is found that maximum number of deliveries i.e. 117 (74%) were conducted by relatives, who include either mother or mother-in-law of the women, followed by 26 i.e. 16 per cent women were delivered by '*Dai*'. (Traditional Birth Attendant).

Table 5.2

Caste-wise place of medical treatment

Sr. No.	Place of treatment	Caste								Total	
		Wadar		Laman		Beldar		Tirumal			
		No.	%	No.	%	No.	%	No.	%	No.	%
1.	PHC	0	0	0	0	0	0	0	0	0	0
2.	Sub Centre	0	0	0	0	0	0	0	0	0	0
3.	Rural hospital	0	0	0	0	0	0	0	0	0	0
4.	Private clinic/hospital	62	42	50	34	31	21	5	3	148	100
5.	Municipal Hospital	2	100	0	0	0	0	0	0	2	100
6.	Government Hospital	8	16	19	38	20	40	3	6	50	100
7.	Traditional Medical Practitioner	0	0	0	0	0	0	0	0	0	0
8.	Any other place	0	0	0	0	0	0	0	0	0	0
	Total	72	36	69	34	51	25.5	8	4	200	100

Table 5.3

Place of deliveries

Sr. No.	*Place*	*Caste*								*Total*	
		Wadar		*Laman*		*Beldar*		*Tirumal*			
		No.	*%*	*No.*	*%*	*No.*	*%*	*No.*	*%*	*No.*	*%*
1.	At home	55	44	38	30	27	22	5	4	125	100
2.	P.H.C.	0	0	0	0	0	0	0	0	0	0
3.	Sub Centre	0	0	0	0	0	0	0	0	0	0
4.	Rural hospital	0	0	0	0	0	0	0	0	0	0
5.	Private clinic/hospital	4	67	0	0	2	33	0	0	6	100
6.	Municipal Hospital	3	37.5	2	25	3	37.5	0	0	8	100
7.	Government Hospital	0	0	0	0	5	100	0	0	5	100
8.	Any other Place	0	0	0	0	0	0	0	0	0	0
9.	N.A.	0	0	8	80	2	20	0	0	10	100
	Total	**62**	**40**	**48**	**31**	**39**	**25**	**5**	**3**	**154**	**100**

Table 5.4

Personnel Conducting Deliveries

Sr. No.	*Personnel*	*Caste*								*Total*	
		Wadar		*Laman*		*Beldar*		*Tirumal*			
		No.	*%*	*No.*	*%*	*No.*	*%*	*No.*	*%*	*No.*	*%*
1.	Gynaecologist	1	2	0	0	2	5	0	0	3	2
2.	Paediatrician	2	3	0	0	3	7	0	0	5	3
3.	Nurse	3	5	2	4	3	7	0	0	8	5
4.	A.N.M.	0	0	0	0	0	0	0	0	0	0
5.	Trained mid-wife	0	0	0	0	0	0	0	0	0	0
6.	Dai	8	12	10	22	6	15	2	29	26	16
7.	Relatives (mother/in-law)	51	78	34	74	27	66	5	71	117	74
	Total	**65**	**100**	**46**	**100**	**41**	**100**	**7**	**100**	**159**	**100**

Status of Abortion

The Table 5.5 shows caste-wise status of abortion of stone quarry workers. From the table it is evident that out of 150, 7 i.e. 5 per cent of the women undergone abortion and 136 i.e. 90 per cent have not undergone the abortion; while 7 i.e. 5 per cent of them are unmarried i.e. they are without spouse, hence the question of abortion does not arise. Out of 62 Wadar 4 (6%) have undergone abortion. Out of 51 Laman 3 (6%) have undergone abortion.

Table 5.5

Status of abortion

Sr. No.	*Status*	*Caste*								*Total*	
		Wadar		*Laman*		*Beldar*		*Tirumal*			
		No.	*%*	*No.*	*%*	*No.*	*%*	*No.*	*%*	*No.*	*%*
1.	Undergone abortion	4	6	3	6	0	0	0	0	7	5
2.	Not undergone abortion	58	94	41	80	32	100	5	100	136	90
	Total	**62**	**100**	**51**	**100**	**32**	**100**	**5**	**100**	**150**	**100**

Contraceptive Methods Used by Respondents

From the Table 5.6 (*See on next page*) it is evident that out of 150 respondents, 7 i.e. 5 per cent respondents are not married i.e. they are without the spouse, hence this table do not pertain to them. It is surprising to note that remaining 143 i.e. 95 per cent of the married respondents do not use any contraceptive methods.

Status of Family Planning Surgery

Table 5.7 depicts the status of family planning surgery undergone by respondents. It is revealed that out of 150 respondents, 51 i.e. 34 per cent of the respondents have undergone family planning surgery and 92 i.e. 61 per cent of the respondents have not undergone family planning surgery. Remaining 7 i.e. 5 per cent of the respondents are unmarried men without their spouse, hence the questions of family planning surgery doesnot arise.

Among them 44 per cent i.e. 29 per cent have undergone tubectomy and 7 i.e. 5 per cent have undergone laproscopy.

Table 5.6

Contraceptive methods used by respondents

Sr. No.	*Contraceptive method*	*Number*	*Percentage*
1.	Condoms	0	0
2.	Copper T	0	0
3.	Oral pill	0	0
4.	Traditional methods	0	0
5.	Do not use	143	95
6.	N.A.	7	5
	Total	**150**	**100**

Table 5.7

Status of family planning surgery

Sr. No.	*Family planning surgery*	*Number*	*Percentage*
1.	Tubectomy	44	29
2.	Laproscopy	7	5
3.	Vasectomy	0	0
4.	Not undergone	92	61
5.	N.A.	7	5
	Total	**150**	**100**

Caste-wise Status of Family Planning Surgery

Table 5.8 reflects on caste-wise status of family planning surgery among respondents. Out of 62 Wadars, 23 i.e. 37 per cent of respondents undergone tubectomy, while 39 i.e. 63 per cent of them have not undergone family planning surgery. Out of 51 Laman respondents 7 i.e. 14 per cent have undergone tubectomy, 5 i.e. 10% have undergone laproscopy and 32 i.e. 62 per cent have not undergone family planning surgery, while

7 i.e. 14 per cent of them are unmarried which means they are without their spouse, hence the question of family planning surgery does not arise. Out of 32 Beldar respondents, 11 i.e. 34.4 per cent of them have undergone tubectomy, 2 i.e. 6.2 per cent have undergone laproscopy, while remaining 19 i.e. 59.4 per cent of them have not undergone family planning surgery. Out of 5 Tirumal respondents 3 (60%) of them have undergone tubectomy, while 2 (40%) have not undergone family planning surgery.

Table 5.8

Caste-wise status of family planning surgery

Sr. No.	*Surgery*	*Caste*								*Total*	
		Wadar		*Laman*		*Beldar*		*Tirumal*			
		No.	*%*	*No.*	*%*	*No.*	*%*	*No.*	*%*	*No.*	*%*
1.	Tubectomy	23	37	7	14	11	34.4	3	60	44	29
2.	Laproscopy	0	0	5	10	2	62.2	0	0	7	5
3.	Vasectomy	0	0	0	0	0	0	0	0	0	0
4.	Not undergone	39	63	32	62	19	59.4	2	40	92	61
5.	N.A.	0	0	7	14	0	0	0	0	7	5
	Total	**62**	**100**	**51**	**100**	**32**	**100**	**5**	**100**	**150**	**100**

Habits of Respondents

Table 5.9 shows habits or additions of the respondents. Among Wadars maximum i.e. 39 per cent of Wadars are addicted to tobacco chewing followed by 30 per cent of respondents addicted to drinking, 15 per cent of Wadar respondents are having habit of smoking and 10 per cent of them chew Gutka, while 7 i.e. 67 per cent are not addicted to anything. Among Laman the percentage of addiction is 38 per cent tobacco chewing. 29 per cent drinking, 18 per cent chewing Gutka, while 5.3 per cent have habit of smoking bidi or cigarette and 2.2 per cent apply misri, while 7.4 per cent of Lamans do not have any addiction. Addiction of tabacco chewing is prevalent among Beldars also. 43 per cent of the Beldar respondent chew tobacco,

12.3 per cent chews Gutka and 12.3 per cent are addicted to drinking, 18 per cent of the Beldar apply misri, while 6 per cent of them addicted to smoking, and the remaining 8.2 per cent do not consume anything. 40 per cent of Tirumals have habit of tobacco chewing, 30 per cent drinking, 10 per cent of them smoke and 10 per cent are addicted to Gutka chewing, while remaining 10 per cent do not have any addiction.

It is found that 39 per cent of the respondents are addicted to chewing of tobacco, 27 per cent consume alcohol, 13 per cent chew Gutka, 10 per cent of the respondents are addicted to smoking, while 4 per cent of respondents use misri and 7 per cent of respondents do not consume anything.

Table 5.9

A comparative table showing addiction/habits of respondents

Sr. No.	Addiction	Caste								Total	
		Wadar		Laman		Beldar		Tirumal			
		No.	%	No.	%	No.	%	No.	%	No.	%
1.	Misri	0	0	2	2.2	9	18	0	0	11	4
2.	Smoking	19	15	5	5.3	3	6	1	10	28	10
3.	Gutka	13	10	17	18	6	12.3	1	10	37	13
4.	Tobacco	49	39	36	38	21	43	4	40	110	39
5.	Alcohol	38	30	28	29	6	12.3	3	30	75	27
6.	Do not consume	7	6	7	7.4	4	8.2	1	10	19	7
	Total	126	100	95	100	49	100	10	100	280	100

General Deaths Among Stone Quarry Workers

Table 5.10 depicts caste wise number of deaths among the families studied. Table 5.10 shows details.

Thus out of 150 families, there are 29 (19%) families where deaths had occurred.

Table 5.10

Caste wise number of deaths

Sr. No.	*No. of deaths*	*Caste*				*Total*
		Wadar	*Laman*	*Bedar*	*Tirumal*	
		No.	*No.*	*No.*	*No.*	
1.	One	11	6	2	0	19
2.	Two	3	1	3	1	8
3.	Three	1	1	0	0	2
4.	More than three	0	0	0	0	0
	Total	**15**	**8**	**5**	**1**	**29**

NUTRITIONAL ISSUES OF STONE QUARRY WORKERS CHILDREN

Participant observation method and focus group discussion among the stone quarry workers revealed following facts about their nutritional habits and issues:

- **Malnutrition**

Malnutrition among stone quarry children is on the higher side. Quantitative data presented in this chapter on the nutritional status of male and female children in all the four communities studied.

Malnutrition Among Stone Quarry Children

Malnutrition refers to the physical effects on the human body of a dietary intake inadequate in quantity and/or quality (Joshi Shubhangi 1992-5): It is a state in which a prolonged lack of one or more nutrients retards physical development or causes specific clinical disorders such as iron deficiency anaemia, goitre etc. Malnutrition can also be defined as an impairment of health resulting from a deficiency, excess of imbalance of nutrients. It includes under-nutrition and over-nutrition as well.

Some of the characteristics of people suffering from malnutrition are dull lifeless hair, greasy pimpled facial skin, dull eyes, shimphed postures, fatigue and depression are easily evident by their spiritless expression and behaviour and lack of interest in surroundings. (Jain Navinchandra and Tribhuwan Robin, 1996).

Malnutrition Among Boys

Sr. No.	Name	Caste	Age	Sex	Actual weight (Kg.)	Expected weight	Grade
1.	Gopichand Nivrutti Chamkure	Wadar	12	M	32	38.3	N
2.	Piraji Yallappa Manjare	Wadar	8	M	16	27.3	III
3.	Arjun Yallappa Manjare	Wadar	2	M	11	13.4	N
4.	Motiram Ganesh Manjare	Wadar	10	M	26	32.6	I
5.	Raju Ganesh Manjare	Wadar	8	M	24	27.3	N
6.	Ramesh Ganesh Manjare	Wadar	6	M	19	21.9	N
7.	Rahul Uttam Mire	Wadar	1	M	5	10.1	IV
8.	Nagesh Govind Devkate	Wadar	1	M	4	10.1	IV
9.	Rahul Vitthal Chamkure	Wadar	5	M	12	20	II
10.	Nikhil Sambhaji Lashkare	Wadar	9	M	20	29.9	N
11.	Amol Sambhaji Lashkare	Wadar	5	M	14	27.3	I
12.	Vijay Piraji Alkunte	Wadar	9	M	27	48.4	III
13.	Anil Piraji Alkunte	Wadar	8	M	21	27.3	I
14.	Kailash Ram Gore	Wadar	14	M	29	48.4	III
15.	Lav Ram Gore	Wadar	7	M	16	24.5	II
16.	Ankush Ram Gore	Wadar	7	M	14	24.5	III

(Contd...)

Sr. No.	Name	Caste	Age	Sex	Actual weight (Kg.)	Expected weight	Grade
17.	Rahul Saheb Chamkure	Wadar	3	M	12	15.6	I
18.	Ganesh Tukaram Devkate	Wadar	8	M	23	27.3	N
19.	Laxman Dnyanu Shinde	Wadar	8	M	13	27.3	IV
20.	Krishna Dnyanu Shinde	Wadar	2 ½	M	13	14.6	N
21.	Kailas Narayan Edke	Wadar	7	M	18	24.5	I
22.	Vilas Narayan Edke	Wadar	5	M	13	20	II
23.	Ankush Rama Chamkure	Wadar	12	M	30	38.3	II
24.	Sunil Lingu Dagade	Wadar	9	M	25	29.9	N
25.	Ramu Lingu Dagade	Wadar	5	M	15	20	I
26.	Krushna Namdev Manjulwad	Wadar	1	M	7	10.1	II
27.	Karan Chandrakant Vitkar	Wadar	4	M	14	17.7	1
28.	Ajay Pandurang Lashkare	Wadar	5	M	15	20	I
29.	Suraj Sanju Lashkare	Wadar	1 ½	M	9	11.4	I
30.	Manjaji Suresh Mire	Wadar	1 mn	M	1.5	3.4	IV
31.	Abhishek Mahadev Jadhav	Wadar	5	M	13	20	II
32.	Abhijit Mahadev Jadhav	Wadar	1	M	8	10.1	I
33.	Raju Govind Rathod	Wadar	5	M	16	20	I

(Contd...)

Sr. No.	Name	Caste	Age	Sex	Actual weight (Kg.)	Expected weight	Grade
34.	Gurunath Ratan Rathod	Wadar	3	M	12	15.6	I
35.	Raju Rama Rathod	Laman	7	M	22	24.5	N
36.	Jitendra Rama Rathod	Laman	2	M	10	13.4	I
37.	Pratik Rajendra Rathod	Laman	2	M	9	13.4	II
38.	Abhishek Tukaram Chavan	Laman	4	M	13	17.7	I
39.	Mutthu Nilesh Chavan	Laman	2	M	14	13.4	N
40.	Viresh Ramu Jadhav	Laman	5	M	14	200	II
41.	Akash Ramu Jadhav	Laman	3 ½	M	12	16.6	I
42.	Raju Babu Rathod	Laman	1 ½	M	10	11.4	N
43.	Jagnnath Nura Rathod	Laman	6	M	20	21.9	N
44.	Ganesh Ashok Jadhav	Laman	4	M	16	17.7	N
45.	Kirti Umesh Jadhav	Laman	3 ½	M	13	16.6	N
46.	Jagesh Somnath Chavan	Laman	4	M	15	17.7	N
47.	Munesh Hanumant Rathod	Laman	6 m	M	8	7.6	N
48.	Sachin Hanmant Rathod	Laman	6 m	M	5	7.6	II
49.	Akshay Babu Rathod	Laman	8	M	17	27.3	II
50.	Shiva Babu Rathod	Laman	5	M	15	20	I

(Contd...)

Sr. No.	Name	Caste	Age	Sex	Actual weight (Kg.)	Expected weight	Grade
51.	Karan Laxman Pawar	Laman	3 ½	M	13	16.6	N
52.	Kiran Suresh Jadhav	Laman	6	M	19	21.9	N
53.	Prem Suresh Jadhav	Laman	4	M	15	17.7	N
54.	Rohit Suresh Jadhav	Laman	3 m	M	5	5.7	N
55.	Chandrakant Ram Rathod	Lamań	9 yr.	M	29	29.9	N
56.	Shrikant Paraji Mohite	Beldar	2 ½	M	12	14.6	N
57.	Mahesh Raosaheb Mohite	Beldar	1 ½	M	8	11.4	II
58.	Karan Popat Mohite	Beldar	1 ½	M	12	11.4	N
59.	Deepak Sukhdev Mohite	Beldar	5	M	13	20	II
60.	Akash Gorakh Mohite	Beldar	7	M	18	24.5	I
61.	Vaibhav Adinath Pawar	Beldar	4	M	10	17.7	III
62.	Jijesh Narayan Putte	Tirumal	7 m	M	8	9.1	N
63.	Namdev Ashruba Devaibone	Triumal	9	M	18	29.9	III

Malnutrition Among Girls

Sr. No.	Name	Caste	Age	Sex	Actual weight	Expected weight	Grade
1.	Nagabai Nivrutti Chamkure	Wadar	10	F	24	32.6	I
2.	Anita Nivrutti Chamkure	Wadar	8	F	18	27.3	II
3.	Poona Yallappa Manjare	Wadar	5	F	14	20	II
4.	Ujwala Uttam Mire	Wadar	7	F	15	24.5	II
5.	Nanda Uttam Mire	Wadar	5	F	12	20	III
6.	Deepali Uttam Mire	Wadar	2	F	8	13.4	III
7.	Nikita Balu Mire	Wadar	2 ½	F	11	14.6	I
8.	Sujata Balu Mire	Wadar	1	F	7	10.1	II
9.	Dnyaneshwari Govind Devkate	Wadar	3	F	9	15.6	III
10.	Asara Vitthal Chamkure	Wadar	6 m	F	5	7.6	I
11.	Maya Sambhaji Lashkare	Wadar	14	F	33	48.4	II
12.	Sangita Piraji Alkunte	Wadar	6	F	19	21.9	N
13.	Gangu Ram Gore	Wadar	10	F	16	32.6	IV
14.	Rajnandini Piraji Yemulwad	Wadar	2 m	F	6	3.4	N
15.	Rekha Tukaram Devkate	Wadar	5	F	13	20	II

(Contd...)

Sr. No.	Name	Caste	Age	Sex	Actual weight	Expected weight	Grade
16.	Kalpana Rohidas Ingle	Wadar	5	F	18	20	N
17.	Nirmala Rohidas Ingle	Wadar	3	F	12	15.6	I
18.	Sujata Rohidas Ingle	Wadar	1 ½	F	10	11.4	N
19.	Surekha Dyanu Shinde	Wadar	6	F	20	21.9	N
20.	Mukta Narayan Edke	Wadar	2	F	13	13.4	N
21.	Kalubai Narayan Edke	Wadar	6 m	F	9	7.6	N
22.	Surekha Rama Chamkure	Wadar	14	F	35	48.4	I
23.	Sunita Lingu Dagade	Wadar	8	F	20	27.3	I
24.	Rupa Namdev Manjulwad	Wadar	6	F	16	21.9	N
25.	Deepa Namdev Manjulwad	Wadar	4	F	11	17.7	II
26.	RenukaChandrakant Vitkar	Wadar	6	F	18	21.9	N
27.	Shanta Shamrao Chamkure	Wadar	14	F	57	48.4	N
28.	Lalita Ratan Rathod	Laman	9	F	18	29.9	III
29.	Yashoda Ratan Rathod	Laman	4	F	15	17.7	N
30.	Sarita Rama Rathod	Laman	9	F	24	29.9	I
31.	Nirmala Ramesh Rathod	Laman	2	F	13	134	N
32.	Kaveri Tukaram Chavan	Laman	2	F	8	13.4	III

(Contd...)

Sr. No.	Name	Caste	Age	Sex	Actual weight	Expected weight	Grade
33.	Laxmi Ramu Jadhav	Laman	9	F	19	29.9	II
34.	Vijya Ramu Jadhav	Laman	7	F	17	24.5	II
35.	Laxmi Nura Rathod	Laman	4 ½	F	15	18.8	I
36.	Savitri Ashok Jadhav	Laman	2	F	13	13.4	N
37.	Laxmi Ashok Jadhav	Laman	1	F	9	10.1	N
38.	Kaveri Umesh Jadhav	Laman	5	F	16	20	I
39.	Motibai Umesh Jadhav	Laman	2	F	11	13.4	N
40.	Sunita Shantilal Rathod	Laman	11	F	29	35.2	N
41.	Savita Shantilal Rathod	Laman	7	F	16	24.5	II
42.	Kamla Shantilal Rathod	Laman	10	F	26	33.9	I
43.	Chendu Hanmant Rathod	Laman	2	F	9	13.4	II
44.	Sonali Chandar Rathod	Laman	3	F	11	15.6	II
45.	Anjali Ram Pawar	Laman	1	F	8	10.1	I
46.	Sonali Laxman Pawar	Laman	5	F	15	20	I
47.	Saloni Laxman Pawar	Laman	1 ½	F	9	11.4	I
48.	Priyanka Raosaheb Mohite	Beldar	10	F	25	33.9	I
49.	Preeti Raosaheb Mohite	Beldar	5	F	14	20	II

(Contd...)

Sr. No.	Name	Caste	Age	Sex	Actual weight	Expected weight	Grade
50.	Pooja Popat Mohite	Beldar	7	F	27	24.5	N
51.	Swatu Naritu /Sakybje	Beldar	9	F	24	29.9	N
52.	Pratiksha Maroti Salunke	Beldar	6	F	16	21.9	I
53.	Diksha Maroti Salunke	Beldar	3	F	13	15.6	N
54.	Chakuli Gorakh Mohite	Beldar	3	F	11	15.6	II
55.	Deepali Gorakh Mohite	Beldar	8 m	F	4	7.6	IV
56.	Varsha Rangnath Devaibone	Tirumal	1½	F	8	11.4	II
57.	Gangasagar Rangnath Devuibone	Tirumal	5	F	13	20	I
58.	Arati Dnyanoba Jagdale	Tirumal	1 ½	F	11	11.4	N

Analysis

The nutritional status as reflected in the tables above has been analysed using the weight for age criteria adopted by the Indian Academy of Paediatrics. Weights for age measurements have been taken here because they are more reliable in terms of accuracy in recording measurements by non-professional staff. A chart developed by the Indian Academy of Paediatrics, published in his book captioned '*A Textbook of Paediatrics*' by Suraj Gupte (1995: 116) was used to grade the degree of Malnutrition among the children of stone-quarry workers. Tables given below also present gender and caste-wise undernourishment gradations.

The nutritional status of 121 children as given (Table 5.11) below reflects the analysis of degree of malnutrition among these children. Out of 121 stone-quarry children measured 64 per cent were malnourished. Of these 14 per cent were severely malnourished. These conclusions are derived from actual weight measurements taken during the fieldwork. The process of analysis and interpretation was done under the guidance of Dr. Vandana Kakrani Associate Professor, Preventive and Social Medicine, B. J. Medical College. We felt that there is a need for conducting a detailed survey among both women as well as children of the stone-quarries, so as to assess their nutritional status. Furthermore, it is also recommended, that studies by medical scientists by carried out on occupational health of stone-quarry workers.

Table 5.13 reveals that, the Wadar children showed maximum degree of malnutrition i.e. 71 per cent followed by Beldar children. 64 per cent, then the Tirumal children 60 per cent and lastly the Laman children 56 per cent. Thisindicates that the Lamans eat better food than the other three communities.

Table 5.14 is self-explanatory and reveals percentage of caste-wise undernourished children. In their report captioned 'Malnutrition related deaths of tribal children', in Nandurbar, Bhatia Arun and Tribhuwan Robin (2002:8) used similar methodology to assess the nutritional status of 136 siblings of deceased children in Nandurbar district and revealed that 76.5 per cent of the siblings were malnourished. Of these 40 per cent were suffering from severe malnourishment.

Table 5.11

Degree of Malnourishment in 121 children

Sr. No.	*Gradation*	*Sex*				*Total*	
		Male		*Female*			
		Number	*%*	*Number*	*%*	*Number*	*%*
1.	Normal	24	38	19	33	43	36
2.	Grade I Mild Malnourishment (Body wt. between 70% to 80% of the expected weight for that age)	17	27	16	28	33	27
3.	Grade II Moderate Malnourishment (Body weight 60% to 70%)	12	19	16	28	28	23
4.	Grade III Severe Malnourishment (Body weight 50% to 60%)	06	9.5	05	08	11	09
5.	Grade IV Severe Malnourishment (Body weight below 50%)	04	6.3	02	03	06	05
	Total	**63**	**100**	**58**	**100**	**121**	**100**

Table 5.12

Gender wise difference in the level of Malnutrition

Sr. No.	*Grade*	*Sex*				*Total*	
		Male		*Female*			
		Number	*%*	*Number*	*%*	*Number*	*%*
1.	Normal	2.4	38	19	33	43	36
2.	Grades I and II	29	46	32	56	61	50
3.	Grades III and IV	10	16	7	11	17	14
	Total	**63**	**100**	**58**	**100**	**121**	**100**

Table 5.12 reveals that out of 121 children, the degree of malnutrition was found to be equal (i.e. 3.9%) between both genders.

- **High Intake of Carbohydrates**

It was observed that the stone worker communities consume large quantities of carbohydrate food, such as rice, jowar, bajra, wheat and maize roti (bread). Secondly, consumption of foods having proteins, minerals, vitamins, oils and fats is less or absent in their daily diet.

- **Government Nutrition Programme**

It was observed that both the stone quarry sites studied, did not have any nutrition supplement programe implemented by the Government of Maharashtra.

- **Nutrition Programme by NGO**

An NGO by the name '*Santulan*', based in Pune in its report for the years 1997 to 2005 on Page No. 13 stated that the NGO implements Mid-day Meal Programme in Pune District Quarries for 1500 children. In each stone quarry units, trained cooks are appointed, who prepare fixed menu from Monday to Saturday. The mid-day meal consists of cooked rice and various types of pulses and gram. The report however does not reveal the sources of funding for the said programme.

Table 5.13

Cast-wise degree of Malnourishment in 121 children

Sr. No.	*Gradation*	*Sex*								*Total*	
		Wadar		*Laman*		*Belder*		*Tirumal*			
		No.	*%*	*No.*	*%*	*No.*	*%*	*No.*	*%*	*No.*	*%*
1.	Normal	17	29	19	44	05	36	02	40	43	36
2.	Grade I Mild Malnourishment (Body wt. between 70% to 80% of the expected weight for that age)	16	27	13	30	03	21	01	20	33	27
3.	Grade II Moderate Malnourishment (Body weight 60% to 70%)	14	24	09	21	04	29	01	20	28	23
4.	Grade III Severe Malnourishment (Body weight 50% to 60%)	07	12	02	05	01	07	01	20	11	09
5.	Grade IV Severe Malnourishment (Body weight below 50%)	05	08	0	0	01	07	0	0	06	05
	Total	**59**	**100**	**43**	**100**	**14**	**100**	**05**	**100**	**121**	**100**

Table 5.14

Caste wise difference in levels of Malnutrition

Sr. No.	Grade	Caste								Total	
		Wadar		Laman		Beldar		Tirumal			
		No.	%	No.	%	No.	%	No.	%	No.	%
1.	Normal	17	29	19	44	05	36	02	40	43	36
2.	Grades I & II	30	51	22	51	07	50	02	40	61	50
3.	Grades III & IV	12	20	02	05	02	14	01	20	17	14
	Total	**59**	**100**	**43**	**100**	**14**	**100**	**05**	**100**	**121**	**100**

- **Research on Nutritional Status of Stone Quarry Workers**

Interviews with stone quarry supervisors, owners and the workers themselves revealed that there is no research done on the nutritional status of stone quarry workers, especially the Yewalewadi and Moshi quarries studied by us.

ENVIRONMENTAL ISSUES

Impact of Pollution

Quarrying not only pollutes human bodies especially of those working in there but also pollutes environment on large scale. It lays extensive dust on land and water resources, leading to fundamental changes in local environments and biodiversity.

Quarries are often situated in remote areas. The establishment of new quarries generally involves setting up the infrastructure to open up an area as well as the establishment of mining villages for migrant workers, etc. Open pit quarrying involves land excavation, the removal of top-soil and the blasting of soil and surface rock. These activities tend to cause fundamental changes to the natural environment and local ecosystems, ranging from deforestation and the diversion of river-beds to the destruction of flora and fauna etc. In addition, deforestation, quarrying may cause soil erosion and increase flooding during rainy season. Flooding as a result of sand quarrying has been reported to occur regularly (article *Business Line* 2001, Janardhanam, 2002).

The Environmental Investigation Agency (EIA) has published a report on highlighting the destruction of tiger habitat in India, due to (illegal) mining in protected areas. Wildlife experts in India report that at least 200 of India's' protected areas have been impacted in one-way or another by the effects of illegal mining (EIA: 2002).

Dust pollution from quarrying operations tends to affect local air quality (particulate matter). A quarry not only pollutes the air, but may also lead to serious health problems. Dust emissions tend to affect animals, vegetation and agriculture. (Netherlands Committee for IUCN, 1996). However, incidences of animals inhailing dust containing dangerous (silica) substances have been recorded as well as oxygen deprivation of plants and trees which may lead to a plant disease called 'asphyxia' (World Rainforest Movement, 2004). An Indian study observed that dust falling on agricultural crops or tree leaves affected their growth and reduced the plants' capacity for photosynthesis. A study on Karnataka region showed suspended dust particles up to distance of 200 metres (NISM, 2004).

Noise pollution is another common feature of quarrying operations. In addition to adverse health effects in humans, noise pollution can also disrupt fauna. However, no studies adequately assessing the impact on local fauna would be found.

In the processing of natural stone (sawing and cutting of blocks into slabs or tiles), the production of solid waste at the quarrying site can also be extensive. A study on solid waste generation and utilisation in the stone industry quotes an estimated production of 125 million tones of natural stone generating and estimated 17.8 million tones of solid calcareous waste per annum. This waste constitutes serious environmental hazard, adversely affecting the fertility of the soil, contaminating water sources and contributing to drainage problems (TIFAC, 1999). Farmers living close to stone quarries in Yevalewadi area of Pune city complained that the dust and smoke of the stone-quarries settles on their crops.

Water Consumption

Contrary to processing, the extraction of natural stone is generally not very water intensive. However, extraction (digging) may to a certain extent influence ground water levels. This goes for marble quarries in particular, as these can reach depths, well below ground water levels. In addition water sprays may be used for dust control during transport and general quarrying operations. The increase in water consumption may lead to alterations in the local water economy. A study on the environmental impact of marble mines in the Nagaur district in Rajasthan ranked the impact of quarrying on water resources as significant, although it did not indicate the ways in which quarrying affects the water levels. Disturbance of the local water economy may have a range of environmental and soil consequence including:

- Impact on Biodiversity
- Threats to agricultural and farming activities
- Social conflicts over water sources (EIA, 2002).

Housing and Settlement Environment

Table 4.63 in Chapter 4,depicts the type of ownership of house of the respondents. It suggests that out of 150 respondents studied, 147 i.e. 98 per cent respondents live in the houses provided by quarry owners. Table 4.68 in Chapter 4 suggests that out of 150 respondents, 140 i.e. 93 per cent respondents' houses are of area less than 200 sq.ft.Table 4.70 in chapter four reveals that 90 per cent of the houses of the stone quarry workers are inadequate.

The study has also revealed that the respondents who are stone quarry workers all of them i.e. 150 are migrant workers and maximum of them i.e. 66 per cent are landless.

According to report by CREM, India Committee of Netherlands and SOMO, 2000 migrant workers (and their families) are sometimes provided accommodation at the quarry but, of the most single type rooms for migrant workers are provided for free.

During the fieldwork, it has been also found that the houses provided by the quarry owners are either close to the quarry or nearby crushing machines. Quarries and stone crushers surround some of the settlements. Due to this kind of surrounding even in their houses respondents are continuously get exposed to dust, which is very dangerous to their health.

Although accommodation has been provided by quarry owners, drinking water, electricity and other facilities such as schools, child care, and medical facilities are absent. Houses provided by the quarry owners are without bathrooms and toilets.

Water Scarcity and Hygiene

Informal discussion with the respondents revealed that there is no any water source available in the area they are living. Quarry owners provide water to them through water tankers. During summer season the situation becomes worst. It is also observed that, they bring water from the nearby area, where urban people have settled. For this, they have to go 3 to 4 kilometers away from their houses. Some stone quarry workers also told that sometimes they have to use pond water not only for washing purpose, but also for drinking. This has adverse effect on their health.

Water scarcity gives rise to hygiene problems. As mentioned earlier the houses provided by quarry owners are very small. Bathroom and toilet facilities are not available. Their bathrooms are outside their houses, which are covered only from three sides, either by cloth, plastic sheets, and tin sheets or stones whatever is available to them. There is no proper drainage system. Water used for bath and washing clothes and utensils gets stored near their houses and which can prove harmful to their health and it is also not hygienic.

DISCUSSIONS

Both quantitative and qualitative data presented in the form of statistics and case studies reveal that the stone quarry workers face from following health, nutritional and environmental problems.

Health Problems

— Major and minor accidents and injuries.

— Debts due to loan from moneylenders on heavy interest for medical treatment.

— No health and medical insurance plans for stone quarry workers.

— No compensation policy for reimbursement of medical bills.

— Loss of life at work due to land slides, blasts etc. have no compensation policy.

— No maternity benefits.

— No health check-ups.

— Lack of proper health facilities at the camps.

Nutritional Problems

— Lack of awareness of nutrition, education and balanced diet.

— Higher intake of carbohydrates.

— Incidence of malnutrition among children and women is high.

(c) Environmental Problems

— Problem of pollution due to dust and smoke at the quarries poses threats of respiratory disorders.

— Unhygienic conditions due to drainage, dust, smoke, children defecating in the camps, adults urinating near the tents or in the temporarily built plastic bathrooms.

— Dust settles on utensils, food, and water of the quarry workers.

— Nearby farmers complain about dust setting on crops and vegetables.

6

SOCIAL INSECURITY AMONG STONE QUARRY WORKERS

SOCIAL INSECURITY

On the lines of studies by Jan Breman (1996) and Tribhuwan Robin and Andreassen (2003) regarding the concept of social insecurity, an attempt has been made to present the issues of social insecurity among the stone quarry workers. In the metropolitan cities the corporate sectors provide social, health, nutritional, environment and economic security to their officers as well as workers. However, the stone quarry workers are deprived of the above facilities.

HEALTH INSECURITY

Table 6.1 depicts the status of provision of facilities during sickness to the workers from quarry owner. From the table given below, it is evident that out of 150 respondents no one has received any facility of first aid treatment, special diet, and medical aid from quarry company doctor, medical allowance and medi-claim policy. The stone quarry owners really do not bother to think of health insurance of workers. Table 6.1 (*See on next page*) provides the health insecurity status of the respondents.

MATERNITY BENEFITS

Table 6.2, reflects on the facilities provided to women during their pregnancy by the quarry owner. It is evident from the table that all 150 respondents have responded negatively.

Women who work on stone quarry do not receive any facilities during pregnancy such as iron and calcium tablets, nutritious food, medical check-up, maternity leave and immunization. Quarry owners do not provide above mentioned facilities. Contrary to what is happening to the stone quarry women, the corporate and Government Departments offer ample maternity benefits such as 3 to 6 months leave, financial assistance etc.

Table 6.1

Health facilities by quarry owner

Sr. No.	*Facilities during sickness*	*Provided*	*Not provided*
		No.	*No.*
1.	First aid treatment	0	150
2.	Special diet	0	150
3.	Medical aid from quarry company doctor	0	150
4.	Medical allowance	0	150
5.	Medi-claim policy	0	150

Table 6.2

Maternity benefits

Sr. No.	*Maternity benefits*	*Status*	
		Received	*Not received*
1.	Iron and calcium tables	0	150
2.	Nutritious food for pregnant women	0	150
3.	Medical check-up	0	150
4.	Maternity leave	0	150
5.	Immunisation	0	150

NUTRITIONAL INSECURITY

Table 6.4 depicts the status of provision of nutrition facilities by quarry owner. It is seen from the table, that out of 150 respondents no one has received nutrition facility such as nutrition supplements, canteen with subsidized rates and subsidised grocery shop, as not a single quarry has provided above mentioned nutrition facilities.

Table 6.3

Nutritional security

Sr. No.	*Nutrition facilities*	*Status*	
		Received	*Do not received*
1.	Nutrition supplement	0	150
2.	Canteen with subsidised rates	0	150
3.	Subsidised grocery	0	150

Corporate sectors ensure that their workers get breakfast, lunch and tea at subsidized rates. This is an extra incentive and security to the workers. On the contrary, neither stone quarry workers nor their children get any nutritional supplements from the owner.

ECONOMIC INSECURITY

Table 6.4 shows the status of provision of economic security to the quarry workers provided by quarry owner. From the table given below, it is seen that out of 150 respondents no one has received benefit of provident fund, gratuity, pension or festival bonus, as not a single quarry owner has provided above-mentioned economic facilities.

Table 6.4

Economic security

Sr. No.	*Economic security*	*Status*	
		Provided	*Not provided*
		No.	*No.*
1.	Provident fund	0	150
2.	Gratuity	0	150
3.	Pension	0	150
4.	Festival bonus	0	150

Working for stone quarry owners without any economic security for life after retirement and while working is the only means of livelihood.

CIVIC AMENITIES

Table 6.5 reflects on status of provision of civic amenities provided by quarry owners to the quarry workers. It is seen that quarry owners have not provided basic civic amenities such as regular water supply, electricity, public toilets, bathrooms and drainage system. Out of 150 respondents, no one has received above mentioned facility.

Table 6.5

Civic amenities

Sr. No.	*Civic amenities*	*Status*	
		Receive	*Did not received*
		Number	*Number*
1.	Regular water	0	150
2.	Electricity	0	150
3.	Public toilet and bathroom facility	0	150
4.	Drainage system	0	150

Since the stone quarry workers live in an area owned by private owners, Government organisations be they Zilla Parishad in rural area and Corporations or municipal councils in the urban areas, do not provide any civic amenities to the stone quarry workers.

BENEFIT RECEIVED FROM GOVERNMENT SCHEMES

Table 6.6 shows benefit of government schemes received by the respondents. From the table given below it is evident that out of 150 respondents not a single respondent have received the benefit of Government schemes, such as ICDS, Balwadi, and Z.P.school, sub centre, PHC, electricity, ration shop, drinking water facility, housing facility or educational scholarship.

Table 6.6

Status of Government schemes

Sr. No.	*Scheme*	*Received*	*Not received*
		Number	*Number*
1.	I.C.D.S.	0	150
2.	Balwadi	0	150
3.	Z.P.school	0	150
4.	P.H.C.	0	150
5.	Sub Centre	0	150
6.	Electricity	0	150
7.	Ration shop	0	150
8.	Drinking water facility	0	150
9.	Housing scheme	0	150
10.	Water tap	0	150
11.	Educational scholarship	0	150
12.	Others	0	150

AVAILABILITY OF DOCUMENTS

Table 6.7 depicts the status of availability of important documents of the respondents. The study has revealed that, out of 150 respondents, 28 i.e. 19 per cent of the respondents do not have any document; while 122 i.e.81 per cent of them have documents with them. Out of 62 Wadars 21 i.e. 34 per cent of them do not have any documents, while remaining 41 i.e. 66 per cent of them have documents. 49 (96%) Laman respondents, out of 51, possess documents, while only 2 (4%) of them do not have any document. Out of 32 Beldar respondents, 27 i.e. 84 per cent of them have important documents, while 5 i.e. 16 per cent of the Beldar respondents do not possess any document, while all 5 Tirumal respondents have at least one document with them.

Table 6.7

Availability of documents

Sr. No.	*Availability status*	*Caste*								*Total*	
		Wadar		*Laman*		*Beldar*		*Tirumal*			
		No.	*%*	*No*	*%*	*No.*	*%*	*No*	*%*	*No.*	*%*
1.	Available	41	66	49	96	27	84	5	100	122	81
2.	Not available	21	34	2	4	5	16	0	0	28	19
	Total	**62**	**100**	**51**	**100**	**32**	**100**	**5**	**100**	**150**	**100**

Note: Documents such as ration card, election card, identify cards, birth certificates, death certificates etc. are considered. In the light of this, Table 6.8 reveals caste-wise status of one or more documents available and respondents who do not have any documents.

CASTE-WISE TYPES OF DOCUMENTS AVAILABLE

Table 6.8 shows documents available with the respondents. From the table it is evident that 27 per cent of the total respondents are ration card holders, 20 per cent of them have house property papers, 16 per cent of them have land documents and 16 per cent of them are election card holders, 10 per cent of them have school/college leaving certificates, 7 per cent respondents are identity card holders, 3 per cent are having birth certificate of their children, while only 1 per cent respondents have bank book (passbook).

Table given below also depicts caste wise available documents with the respondents. Among Wadars, 36 per cent of them are ration card holders, 26 per cent of Wadar respondents have election cards, 23 per cent of them have house property papers and 7.3 per cent are identity card holders, 4.4 per cent of them have school leaving certificate, while 1.5 per cent have bank book and 1.5 per cent have land documents. It is very much clear from the table that among Laman respondents maximum i.e. 30 per cent of them have land documents compared to other three caste groups. 24 per cent of them are ration card holders, 22 per cent of them have house property papers, 14 per cent of them are election card holders, and 8 per cent of them have school leaving certificate, while 2 per cent have birth certificate of their children. Out of total Beldar respondents 23 per cent of the respondents have ration card, 16 per cent of them are identity card holders, 21 per cent of them have school or college leaving certificates, 15 per cent of the Beldar respondents have house property papers, election card holders are 11 per cent while 10 per cent of the Beldar respondents have birth certificate of their children remaining 2 per cent of them have land documents and 2 per cent are having bank book. Among Tirumal respondents 23 per cent of the respondents have ration card and 23 per cent respondents have land documents, 31 per cent are identity card holders, 15 per cent of them have school leaving certificates, while 8 per cent have election card. Informal interviews with respondents reveal that documents such as ration card, election card, land records etc. are kept in their native place. It was observed that very few stone quarry workers keep their documents at the quarry house.

Table 6.8

Caste wise types of documents possessed

Sr. No.	*Document*	*Caste*								*Total*	
		Wadar		*Laman*		*Beldar*		*Tirumal*			
		No.	*%*	*No.*	*%*	*No.*	*%*	*No.*	*%*	*No.*	*%*
1.	Ration card	25	36	28	24	14	23	3	23	70	27
2.	Election card	18	26	17	14	7	11	1	8	43	16
3.	Identify card	5	7.3	0	0	10	16	4	31	19	7
4.	Birth certificate	0	0	3	2	6	10	0	0	9	3
5.	Marriage certificate	0	0	0	0	0	0	0	0	0	0
6.	Death certificate	0	0	0	0	0	0	0	0	0	0
7.	Bank book	1	1.5	0	0	1	2	0	0	2	1
8.	School/college leaving certificate of self/children	3	4.4	9	8	13	21	2	15	27	10
9.	Land documents	1	1.5	36	30	1	2	3	23	41	16
10.	House property papers	16	23	26	22	9	15	0	0	51	20
	Total	**69**	**100**	**119**	**100**	**61**	**100**	**13**	**100**	**262**	**100**

EDUCATIONAL INSECURITY

Table 6.9 given below shows the status of provision of educational facilities provided by quarry owner for the children. From the table given below it is very clear that there is no provision of pre-school, vocational training, higher education facility is made by quarry owners for the children of quarry workers.

At Moshi and Yewalewadi children are going to schools, which are run by an NGO, by the name '*Santulan*'. These schools are known as '*Pashan Shala*' as they are situation near the quarries.

Table 6.9

Educational Insecurity

Sr. No.	*Educational facility*	*Provided*	*Not provided*
		Number	*Number*
1.	Pre-school programme	0	150
2.	Vocational training	0	150
3.	Higher education facility	0	150
4.	Other trainings	0	150

DISCUSSIONS

Both qualitative and quantitative data on the stone quarry workers reveal that the owners of quarries do not provide economic, educational, nutritional, health and environmental securities including civic amenities to the degraded bread-winners. It seems that the quarry owners employ poor, insecured workers whose native places are far away from the stone quarry sites.

Breman Jan (1996) has stated that the quarry owners never employ local people. They prefer to have labourers of caste groups that are associated with stone work profession. In doing so, the stone quarry workers are safe and secure from local politics and problems.

In the interest of getting more profit by employment of cheap labour, the stone quarry owners play with the emotion of stone quarry workers. Few incentives to few smart and dynamic workers are given. These incentives are housing facility, water tanker once a week for the labourers etc. The stone quarries really do not provide any security to the workers, except few incentives to make the work for his personal profit.

On the other hand, Government and NGOs, like '*Santulan*' are doing a bit for the stone quarry workers. The NGO called '*Santulan*' is providing education to stone quarry children. The NGO is also engaged in formation SHGs and implementing other programmes. To conclude, NGOs are certainly trying to provide social security to the stone workers certainly.

SOCIAL, ECONOMIC, LEGAL, HEALTH, NUTRITIONAL ETC. INSECURITIES: CASE STUDIES

Statistical data and tables in Chapters 4, 5 and 6 reveal quantitative facts of social, economic, legal, political, health, nutritional, housing etc. insecurities among the stone quarry workers. This section of Chapter Six presents qualitative data in the form of case studies. Ten case studies on social insecurity among the stone quarry workers have been given. Interpretation and analysis of both quantitative and qualitative data only reveals one thing and that is the degree of insecurity in various spheres social life is very high.

Case Study No. 1

Aim of the Case Study

To highlight the financial insecurities faced by stone quarry workers, while at work on account of serious injuries.

Background

Ganesh Manjare aged 35, a male member of the Wadar caste, a native of Parbhani district in the State of Maharashtra, who currently works as a labourer in Pune at the Moshi village quarry. He has three sons and a daughter. His mother, Bahinabai, who is a widow, lives with him in a temporary house made up of plastic sheets.

Course of Events

Ganesh who was working at a quarry in Parbhani in 2002 met with an accident at the site in Parbhani and got his leg fractured. His sons rushed him to a hospital. It took him one and a half month to recover. He took a loan of Rs. 20,000/- from a moneylender on 25 per cent interest. The stone quarry owner did not pay a penny to Ganesh. In fact, Ganesh is still paying the moneylender who gave money for Ganesh's hospitalisation.

In the year 2005, when he came to Pune to work in Moshi village quarry, he injured his eye and a leg while breaking stones. Here again he borrowed Rs 8,000/- for medication. The owner did give him Rs. 3000/-. Currently, Ganesh is not able to see properly and work effectively due to his leg injury.

Analysis

Ganesh, who fractured his leg while working in Parbhani quarry and wounded his eye and leg at Moshi quarry in Pune, cannot work hard and effectively. He has not been given any medical compensation by the first (Parbhani) quarry owner, while the second owner has not shown any mercy by giving him a lighter kind of job. Like Ganesh, several cases of injuries and accidents occur at the quarries. Fortunately, for such victims, it is the moneylenders, who came to their rescue, and not quarry owners, nor Government, nor N.G.Os.

Case Study No. 2

Aim of the Case Study

To study the impact of serious injuries due to accidents, on the life of a unskilled female quarry worker.

Background

Sagarbai Edke, aged 55, a widow, native of Parbhani district, a member of Wadar caste is living with an unmarried son of her in Moshi village quarry. Since 2004, Sagarbai is living in Moshi. Before coming to Moshi, she was working at Wagholi stone quarry.

Course of Events

During the summer of 2005, Sagarbai met with an accident while loading small lumps of stones. A tractor ran over her right hand and she had an eye injury as well. She was rushed to the hospital by the quarry owner. Out of the total medical expense of Rs. 8000/-, the owner paid her Rs. 5000/-. Sagarbai did recover, but the impact of injuries was part and parcel of her life.

Analysis

As a result of her hand and eye injury, Sagarbai cannot work. She lost her job, means of livelihood and survival. Today she has to depend on her son's income. She has not been given any old age or health security by the quarry owner.

Case Study No. 3

Aim of the Case Study

To unveil the digestive disorders that occurred among the children of the stone-quarry workers by drinking impure and unclean water available within the quarry vicinity.

Background

Sunita, aged 8, daughter of Mathurabai Dagade, belongs to Wadar caste and an inhabitant of Moshi village quarry site, suffered from jaundice.

Course of Events

During the rainy season of 2007, Sunita, a daughter of a quarry worker suffered from jaundice, as a result of drinking unclean and impure water this water was made available by the stone quarry owners, she was admitted in a municipal corporation hospital by her parents for 13 days. The family spent around Rs. 3000/- on her medical care. Secondly, both the parents had to be with the daughter in the hospital as a result of which they were deprived of the daily wages. They borrowed money from moneylenders and relatives.

Analysis

Unavailability of clean and pure drinking water causes digestive disorders among several stone quarry workers and their children. This case reveals that there is an urgent need for the Government and quarry owners to provide clean and pure drinking water to the families living at the quarry sites. Sunita's parents did not receive any medical compensation from quarry owner.

Case Study No. 4

Aim of Case Study

To study the practice of maternity benefits given by the quarry owners to the pregnant women of the labourers.

Background

Sunita Lalman Mohite, aged 33, a mother of three children, a member of Beldar caste, was pregnant during the year 2006.

Course of Events

Sunita who conceived her third child during 2006 was living at the Moshi quarry site. Her son Mahesh, who was born as low birth weight baby was kept in an incubator in the hospital. The family had to pay an amount of Rs. 50,000/- to Rs. 60,000/- for delivery and medication expenses of the new-born. They did not receive any compensation from the quarry owner although Sunita is working for the quarry owner.

Analysis

Like Sunita there are several women who work as daily labourers do not get any maternity benefits from the quarry owners. In this case, the medical and health complications faced by the new-born forced the parents to spent 50,000/- to Rs. 60,000/- which they borrowed on interest.

Case Study No. 5

Aim of the Case Study

To highlight deaths of stone quarry workers, due to landslides.

Background

A local newspaper captioned '*Sakal*' dated 16-6-2007, Pune edition, reported that Mahendra Stone Quarry Company's three workers namely Natthu Appa Pawar, aged 50 years, Tippa Tharu Pawar aged 26 and Shankar Jadhav, aged 24 died on 15-6-2007, when there was a landslide in a quarry owned by Mahendra Stone Company.

Course of Events

On 15-6-2007 when these three workers went to the quarry with the truck to load stones, there was a landslide from a height of 60 to 70 feet, due to which large chunks of rocks that fell on the truck as well as on the three stone-quarry workers, out of which, one was driver.

Analysis

Natural calamities such as landslides during rainy season take away lives of several stone quarry workers. Mr.Devkar, the owner of above said Stone Quarry Company did not provide the three families any financial compensation.

The case study reveals that several stone quarry workers who sacrifice their life for their owners, get deprived of death compensation of their families and also cannot afford to fight legal cases in the Court of Law, by hiring lawyers who charge heavy fees.

Case Study No. 6

Aim of Case Study

To highlight legal insecurities faced by stone-quarry workers on account of injustice done by the quarry-owners.

Background

Dattatray Ashruba Davaibone, 30 years old stone quarry worker, belongs to caste Tirumal. He is an illiterate man, having one son and two daughters. His wife also works on stone-quarry. His native place is Talegaon village in block Ahmadpur of Latur District in Maharashtra. Since the last 10 years, he is living in Moshi.

Course of Events

Dattatray, who became a victim of landslide during the rainy season of 2004, stated that he was breaking big lumps of stones in the quarry when a large stone fell on his head from a height of 10 to 15 feet; as a result there was serious bleeding. He was taken to Desai Hospital, where the doctors treated him for a period of two weeks. The injury was so serious that the doctors had to stitch the cut. As a result of which there were 18 stitches. The total cost of the head injury and its treatment was Rs. 40,000/-. The quarry owner compensated by giving him Rs. 30,000/- for the treatment; while the remaining Rs. 10,000/- were paid by Dattatray.

Furthermore, in April 2007, Dattatray met with another accident while loading the tractor with stones, when a stone fell on his hand which got fractured. Here again Dattatray had to borrow Rs. 3500/- for the treatment. The stone quarry owner did not give him any compensation for second accident.

Analysis

Dattatray, a poor stone quarry worker was deprived of his right over medical claim. Although Dattatray was convinced of the fact that his owner cheated him by not paying the money and that he wanted to sue his owner into the court of law. However, social backwardness, poor literacy background, lack of legal empowerment and utter poverty, deprived Dattatray to revolt against the owner for legal rights. The fear of loosing his job was yet another factor, to remain on the back foot. Thirdly, the fear of loosing his wife's job was yet another reason. Finally, being an unskilled and money wise weak labourer, the favour of giving Dattatray's family a chance to earn as well live at the quarry site by the owner, according to Datta was a boon, that suppressed the thought of legally revolting against the quarry owner.

Case Study No. 7

Aim of the Case Study

To present the problems of personal insecurities faced by young stone-quarry women workers.

Background

Mathurabai Lingu Dagade, aged 28, is a stone-quarry worker, currently working on a quarry at Moshi. She is an illiterate woman having 2 sons and 2 daughters. Her husband is also a stone-quarry worker. She is the member of Wadar caste. She is originally from the village Garegaon in block Purna of District Parabhani in Maharashtra. Since last two years she is living in Moshi with her family.

Course of Events

Mathurabai Lingu Dagade during an informal interview with her stated that, the young girls and women working at the quarries often become victims of lust by men and supervisors due to lack of personal security. She further explained that because she and her family lives in a temporary house, constructed of plastic sheets having an area of 60 sq. feet, she is not able to cook food inside the house nor take bath in it due to lack of space. She complained that young girls and women living in such type of houses often have to take bath in an open space near the tent, wherein they get exposed to the people living around them. She said that, men often stare at them, while taking bath, changing clothes and urinating.

Analysis

Lack of proper housing of bathroom facilities for young girls and women gives rise to personal insecurity, while they have to bath, change clothes, urinate etc.

Case Study No. 8

Aim of the Case Study

To understand the impact of pollution on the health of stone-quarry workers.

Background

Fieldwork of the present study is conducted at Moshi and Yewalewadi quarry sites. Informal interviews of four stone-quarry workers i.e. two from Yewalewadi namely Mallesh

Aarune, aged 50, Manohar Nimbalkar, aged 45 and two from Moshi namely Govind Devkate, aged 26 and Sahebu Chamkure, aged 23, were conducted. Informal interviews were conducted to find out the impact of pollution on the health of stone quarry workers.

Course of Event

During the informal interviews with above mentioned stone-quarry workers, it has revealed that they are suffering from respiratory disorders caused due to pollution at stone-quarries. They also said that stone quarry owners do not provide any safety measures such as earmuffs, dust masks, gloves and shoes to the stone-quarry workers. The houses provided to stone quarry workers are near stone quarries and crushers due to which their houses are dusty. Food and drinking water also gets polluted due to dust.

Analysis

Constant release of dust, stone and cement particles in the air, causes respiratory disorders. Children are worst victims of not only dust particles, but also the smoke in the quarry vicinity. Quarry owners do not give the workers masks, caps for their safety. Hence the degree of respiratory disorders is high, among them.

Case Study No. 9

Aim of the Case Study

To explore the need for nutrition supplement programme for pregnant and lactating mothers, as well as children at stone quarry.

Background

Two stone quarries namely Yewalewadi and Moshi on the outskirts of Pune city were selected to study as to what extent efforts have been made by Government and N.G.Os to provide nutrition supplement to pregnant and lactating mothers and children at the stone quarries.

Course of Events

During our field work, we observed that an N.G.O. by the name *'Santulan'* is running *"Pashan Schools"* for the children of stone quarry workers, however, there is no nutrition supplement programme for the lactating and pregnant women and children as well.

Analysis

The incidence of under-nutrition among stone quarry women and children is high. The environmental hygienic conditions at the quarries are not up to the mark. The consumption of carbohydrate food among the stone workers is high. They are not aware of balanced diet. To add to these problems there is no nutrition supplement programme.

Case Study No. 10

Aim of the Case Study

To study the civic amenities provided to the stone quarry workers by the owners, N.G.Os. and Government.

Background

Both Yewalewadi and Moshi stone quarries were studied to find out what civic facilities and amenities are given to the stone quarry workers.

Course of Events

During our field work of one year i.e. from January to December, 2007, one of the research tasks undertaken was to expose civic amenities and facilities at the quarries.

Analysis

It was observed that in both the quarries, no Government and N.G.Os. are providing any civic amenities and facilities. It is the owners who provide housing facilities to few workers only, while other live in huts and tents. Of course, toilets, urinals and bathrooms are not provided by anybody including the owners. The stone quarry workers go out into the nature for their natural calls.

7

SUMMARY OF FINDINGS, CONCLUSIONS AND RECOMMENDATIONS

SUMMARY

Since the last two decades the processes of development, modernisation and globalisation have invaded the rural areas as well as the psyche of the people.The process of rural-urban migration is rapidly taking place as a result of better employment opportunities in the metropolitan cities. The members of higher caste communities in the rural areas who have access to social, economic and political resources can afford to send their children for higher education and better job opportunities in the cities. With the partnership of the foreign companies, corporate sector and IT sector in the megacities of India have created job opportunities with higher scales of payment. These educated and economically well off youth are provided with internationally recognised social and economic security measures by the employer, company, corporate and IT sector. Similarly those rural youth who get into Government sector also get all the social security benefits.

Well, this is one side of the coin or scenario as regards the rural youth and educated adults who get recruited in organised sectors. Indian caste system hierarchy has created several caste-based occupational categories of labourers, artisans and workers. Some of these poor and unskilled groups never have been part and parcel of an internationally acclaimed organised sector. With the process of rapid industrialisation, urbanisation modernisation and technological development these unskilled, insecured, less empowered, socially stigmatised and depressed poor people find themselves insecured in the main stream of organised sector. This handicap of their socio-economic status and lack of professional skills has been a plus point of the shared employers and small-scale entrepreneurs within and outskirts of the cities who have been successfully exploiting these labourers and workers of the unorganised sectors. In the process of this kind of exploitation, the so called labourers have been deprived of their social, economic and other rights as workers of company or an organisation for which they are working. This research study attempts to unveil the social insecurity among one such unorganised sector namely the stone-quarry and stone-crusher units. Before getting into the actual reality of social insecurity among the stone quarry workers, it would be appropriate at this juncture to present certain theoretical concepts and definitions of terms such as unorganised sector, social security, informal sector and social insecurity by social scientists and more precisely by the Sociologists.

In order to find solutions, for the research questions raised in chapter one by conducting pilot study, through focus group discussions with stone-quarry workers, their supervisors, owners and representatives of NGOs working for rights of stone-workers. Initially three stone quarry sites on the outskirts of the Pune City were visited, so as to develop research tools to gather relevant data.

Finally, we selected two stone quarry sites namely, Yewalewadi, near Kondhwa region situated towards the South-East of Pune City and Moshi, the northern part of Pune City. It was observed that four major communities work as insecured daily wage labourers for the quary owners. These communities are Wadars, Lamans, Beldars and Tirumals. Besides these communities we also explored that members of scheduled castes and nomadic groups also work as labourers at the quarries. Even members of Maratha Caste who do not have land or other resources work there.

Two interview schedules, one for the household head and second for the medical practitioners who practice around the stone-quarry vicinity, were designed, so as to gather relevant data. We selected 150 respondents from both the sites. The sample was selected purposively. The quantitative data was organised systematically keeping in view caste and geographical area indicators. Using Excel software the data was entered, so as to tabulate significant indicators in the form of tables to support the theoretical reflections in this study. Based on the review of literature and pilot study conducted by us, following research questions were developed. These are as follows:

(i) Majority of stone-quarry workers belonged to those castes and/or nomadic groups whose traditional occupations were associated with stone-work, construction and transportation of building material?

(ii) Lower the level of social, educational, economic, political and development awareness, empowerment and status in an individual, family or community, higher the degree of social insecurity?

(iii) Greater the degree of economic insecurity lesser the chance of financial support and loans from banks and financial institutions ?

(iv) Lesser the degree of professional skills and literacy level, higher the degree of exploitation and insecurity in an unorganised sector?

(v) The percentage of hiring migrant and semi-nomadic labourers by stone-quarry owners, rather than local labourers in higher in most of the quarries?

Keeping in view the above theoretical background and research questions, the present study aims to unveil the issues of social insecurity among the stone quarry workers by studying following objectives.

Objectives of the Study

(i) To study the socio-economic and ethnographic background of the stone quarry communities.

(ii) To understand the health, nutritional and environment problems and insecurity faced by stone quarry women and their children.

(iii) To explore social security provided by stone-quarry owners, Government and Non-Government organisations to stone quarry workers, as well as communities themselves.

(iv) To unveil the issues of social insecurity among the stone quarry workers.

(v) To suggest a module of social security for stone quarry workers.

The quantitative and qualitative facts gathered by conducting field work have been scientifically analysed, interpreted and presented in seven chapters. Given below is the sequence of same.

Sr. No.	*Chapter*	*Title*
1.	One	Introduction
2.	Two	Research Methodology
3.	Three	Brief Ethnographic Profile of the Wadars, Lamans, Beldars and Tirumals.
4.	Four	Socio-economic background and stone quarry workers.
5.	Five	Health, Nutritional and Environmental issues of stone quarry workers.
6.	Six	Social Insecurity among stone quarry workers.
7.	Seven	Summary, Conclusions and Recommendations.

Significance of the Study

As mentioned earlier, the term social security is seen as something intrinsically human, in terms of need, value and human right. It is a multi-dimensional phenomenon dealing with different economic, social and political systems, ideologies and theories. Hence at the theoretical level this study will not only be useful in developing theoretical insights to Sociologists, but to Economists, Anthropologists, Development Experts, Social Security Experts and Political Science Researchers as well. The facts and observations reported in the study will certainly be a base for social scientists to develop new theoretical insights and ideologies.

At the more practical level this study will be useful to policy makers and administrators of the Government Departments, Social Injustice and Empowerment etc. so as to evolve social security plans and development programmes for the stone quarry workers. The study will be useful to NGOs and activists working for stone quarry workers as well.

FINDINGS

As mentioned earlier, the findings, theory and methodology of the present study is presented in seven chapters. The first three chapters deal with introduction of concepts and definitions about social security, social insecurity, unorganised sector, informal sector, the types of labourers that befall within the unorganised sector and sociological view of the informal sector by Jan Breman. The first chapter also presents objectives of study, research questions and its significance, second chapter captioned 'Research Methodology' presents the techniques and methods used by us to scientifically gather, analyse, interprets and present relevant quantitative and qualitative data. The third chapter gives a brief ethnographic profile of the target population.

Chapter four, five and six are data chapters of the study. In this section chapter-wise major findings of the study are presented, in three sections namely:

(A) Socio-economic status of stone quarry workers;

(B) Health, Nutritional and Environmental issues of the stone quarry workers;

(C) Social Insecurity among the stone quarry workers.

To begin with, given below are findings regarding the socio-economic status of the stone quarry workers.

(A) Socio-economic Status of Stone Quarry Workers

It is evident from the primary data presented in Chapter Four on the socio-economic status of all the four communities, that each of the caste group which was traditionally into stone work/business have taken up the same profession despite of the technological advances. With the introduction of new technology such as stone-crushing machines, drilling gadgets, blasting techniques and introduction of trucks etc. the young generation of Wadars, Lamans, Beldars and Tirumals are opting for jobs, such as drivers, crushing machine operators, drill machine operators, tar and stone mixer operators etc. These changes are certainly taking place among these communities. In fact, some of these groups who have settled in slums are working as contractors and dealers in the construction industry.

A comparative analysis of few indicators has been presented in this section of the Chapter. These are as follows:

- **Settlement Pattern and House Types**

Out of all the four communities it was observed that the Wadars lived in plastic sheets tent and tin houses. Out of the total sample of 150 respondents 62 were Wadar respondents. Out of these 62 Wadars, 37 i.e. 60 per cent live in temporary tents made up of plastic sheets; while remaining 14 i.e. 22 per cent live in tin houses and 5 i.e. 8 per cent live houses made up of stone walls and tin roofs; while only 6 i.e. 10 per cent live in houses made up of brick walls and tin or cement sheets roof. Details about settlement pattern and house types of Lamans, Beldars and Tirumals are given in this chapter. The reason why the Wadars live in plastic tents and temporary houses is because of the characteristic nomadic, landlessness and poverty.

- **Educational Status**

Illiteracy rate among the total sample was found to be very high. It was observed that out of 150 respondents, 102 i.e. 68 per cent were illiterate. It was also shocking to note that out of 150 respondents, 133 were males. 115 spouses (females) of the 133 male respondents were illiterate. Furthermore, caste-wise statistics reveal that out of 62 Wadar respondents 48 (i.e. 77%) were illiterate. Similarly, out of the total 51 Laman respondents 34 i.e.67 per cent were illiterate. Out of total 32 Beldars 18 i.e. 56.3 per cent were illiterate. Yet another interesting finding regarding illiteracy status of the spouses of the target population is concerned the facts are as follows. It was observed that 58 i.e. 100 per cent of Wadar, 38 i.e. 74 per cent of Laman, 16 i.e. 50 per cent of Beldars and 3 i.e. 60 per cent of Tirumals were illiterate.

- **Social Status**

Despite of the rapid urbanisation, modernisation and technological advancement the social position of the Wadars, Lamans, Beldars and Tirumals in the caste hierarchy as viewed by them as well as other caste groups remains the same. They are still branded as caste communities associated with stone, construction and transportation work. Constitutionally all these communities have been listed in the nomadic communities of Maharashtra's schedule list. This social status was and is part of their social life despite of the social changes and occupational shifts that have come into these communities. Their settlement patterns and community solidarity at the quarries are distinct features of their social status even at the quarries which are so close to the urban areas and influenced by the urbanisation. Every caste group lives together in separate settlements in a commonly occupied in a quarry or land. Although it is seen that on common big patch of land there are several stone quarry owners having all these three communities, still one gets to see even stone quarry owners who work very closely to each other have these communities staying separately in separate settlement even on a separate patch of land. This proves that caste component is directly influencing community solidarity among the stone quarry workers. Rituals related to festivities and life transition are observed by these communities among themselves. This proves that caste factor promotes and strengthens strong community bonds. As regards interaction with each other there are some aspects where interaction within these groups takes place especially while drinking liquor, gambling, going to the markets etc. whereas inter-caste marriages are prohibited.

- **Economic Status**

(i) Annual Income

Out of 150 respondents studied 74 i.e. 49 per cent of the respondents' income ranges from Rs. 40,000/- to Rs. 60,000/-. This income range is certainly above the Government of India's BPL (Below Poverty Line) norms. This is because, both the spouses along with teenaged youth or married children in case of joint family earn, hence the family's annual income range is above Rs. 20,000/- per annum.

A comparative analysis of the family's income among the four groups, it is seen that income range above Rs. 80,000/- is seen among 28 per cent of Lamans, 18 per cent of Beldars and only 5 per cent of Wadars and none among the Tirumals. Hence again the Wadar show less income level as compared to the other groups.

(ii) Landless and Landholders

Out of 150 respondents studied 66 per cent were landless and 34 per cent were landholders. A comparative analysis of the four groups studied reveals that maximum landless respondents were among Wadars 95 per cent followed by Beldars, 84 per cent.

Caste-wise comparison of landholders highlights that Lamans were maximum landholders followed by Beldars.

The Lamans who are basically from Rajasthan have migrated to sourthern parts of India in Karnataka, Andhra and South of Maharashtra worked for the Nizams once upon a time may have been given land by the Muslim Kings. Secondly, since they have settled in these areas for over 200 to 300 years may be having their forefather's land and house, hence they are different from the other communities. The study also revealed that Lamans have maximum irrigated land; while the Wadars and Beldars possess non-irrigated and waste land.

(iii) Possession of Livestock

Out of 150 respondents interviewed, 19 i.e. 13% respondents possess livestock. A comparative analysis of the four caste groups revealed that out of 19, 17 i.e. 90 per cent are Lamans and 2 i.e. 10 per cent are Wadars, while none of the Beldar and Tirumal possess livestock. As mentioned earlier that maximum Lamans possess agriculture land hence it is but natural that this group also possess livestock.

(iv) Economic Assets

An attempt was done to find out economic assets possessed by the target population. These assets were fan, radio/tape recorder, television, clock, wrist watch, cupboard, mobile, bed, table/chairs, stove, cooking gas connection, bicycle, mobike and other items including mixer, utensils, baskets etc. The immovable assets which are land and house which are prominently found among the Lamans. Out of the movable assets radio/ tape recorders and stoves were found among all the 4 groups. It is also observed that due to mobility and nomadic nature among all the four communities, the degree of possession of movable assets is very less.

(v) Job Status

It was observed that all 150 families working for the stone quarry owners do not have permanent job or any job security. Some of them move within the quarry to work for other quarry owners in case of job crisis.

(vi) Skilled and Unskilled Work

Considering the socio-economic status of Wadars it may be said that the degree of unskilled manpower and labour as high as 90 per cent. While the percentage of skilled manpower/ labour such as stone crusher operators, drivers, drill machine operators, supervisors etc. is high among the Laman and Beldars as their socio-economic status is higher than the Wadars.

(vii) Number of Earning Members

Since all the respondents studied are daily wage labourers and that there is no job security both the spouses work so as to get sufficient income for the family. It was observed that the number of earning members among Wadars followed by Lamans, Beldars and Tirumals.

(viii) Weekly Payment

Greater the economic need and urgency of cash, earlier the payment. All respondents are basically hand to mouth, and are also addicted to alcohol, smoking, chewing tobacco and gutka, gambling hence tend to spend cash immediately. In such cases payments are made weekly. This only points out the insecure and temporary job status of respondents.

(ix) Borrowing Behaviour

It was observed that the percentage of borrowing money in times of crisis from friends and relatives followed by moneylenders.

Facts revealed in Chapter Four about the socio-economic status of the stone quarry workers in general, as well as individual caste groups, reveals that low social, economic, educational, health, nutritional and political profile of the stone quarry workers have made them victims of social insecurity. The quarry owners do provide some with housing security which is temporary is not good enough to secure them.

(B) Health, Nutritional and Environmental Issues of the Stone Quarry Workers

Health

Stone quarry workers from an unorganised sector of industry scattered all over India. There are various procedures and operations involved in this work viz. blasting, drilling, stone-cutting, stone-breaking, loading, crushing, transporting. Based on these operations, the workers are employed at different places as per the nature of work and are exposed to silica dust of different concentrations. (Ghotkar, Maldhure, Zadpey, 1995).

The mining and quarrying sector is traditionally a sector that possesses large risks to occupational health and safety. The most important occupational risks related to stone quarrying include:

- Fatal accidents;

- Physical injuries requiring medical treatments;
- Work related illnesses : respiratory diseases.

Such as silicosis and tuberculosis due to inhalation of dust.

Case Studies

- *Place of Treatment:* It is observed that out of 200; 148 i.e. 74 per cent respondents prefer to go to private doctor for medical treatment.
- *Place of deliveries:* It is seen that, out of 154, 125 i.e. 81 per cent of the women delivered at home.
- *Personnel conducting deliveries:* It is observed that out of 159, 117 i.e. 74 per cent of the deliveries of stone quarry women were conducted by either mother or mother-in-law or relatives, while 26 i.e. 16 per cent of the deliveries were conducted by 'Dai' (Traditional Birth Attendant).
- *Use of contraceptive methods by respondents*: It is surprising to note that out of 150 respondents, 143 i.e. 95 per cent respondents do not use any contraceptive method.
- *Status of family planning surgery:* Out of 150 respondents, 51 i.e. 34 per cent of the respondents have undergone family planning operation, while 92 i.e. 61 per cent of them have not undergone family planning operation.
- *Addiction:* Some of the major addictions found among all the four communities were chewing tobacco and gutka (scented tobacco), smoking, drinking alcohol and brushing teeth with tobacco called "*misri*." All the habits mentioned above are seen at a higher rate among the men. It was observed that while interviewing the male respondents especially they were reluctant to disclose the habit of alcoholism. It is observed that the caste-wise percentage of above mentioned habits especially alcohol consumption and chewing tobacco is more or less is same among all caste groups.
- *Health facilities at quarries:* In both the quarries studied no health facilities were provided to the quarry owners by the labourers.

- *Financial support during accidents and injuries:* In times of minor and major accidents at the quarries the labourers meet with small and serious accidents. In some cases the owners do pay one fourth or in some cases half of the amount, as they are afraid that the case may be highlighted by the media. However, there is no policy that envisages the financial guarantee in times of minor or major accidents of the labourers.
- *Death Compensation:* In chapter five, case studies have been presented, that reflect that there is no clear-cut policy of the stone quarry companies for compensation of money to the family members of a labourer who dies while working at the quarry.
- *Malnutrition:* The percentage of the malnutrition among the boys and girls between the age 0 to 14 is 62 and 67 percentage respectively. The percentage of malnutrition among stone quarry women workers between the age 15 to 49 was not reported. Age range-wise tables of both children, males and females, are presented in chapter 5. Other nutritional problems are also presented in Chapter 5.
- *Environment:* Qualitative data gathered regarding the environmental issues faces by stone quarry workers and their families can be classified as follows:
    1. Problems of pollution due to dust and smoke at the quarries posses threats of respiratory disorders;
    2. Unhygienic conditions due to drainage, dust, smoke, children defecating in the camps, adults urinating near the tents or in the temporarily built plastic bathrooms;
    3. Dust settles on utensils, food, and water of the stone quarry workers;
    4. Nearby farmers complain about dust settling on agriculture crops and vegetables.

(C) Social Insecurity Among Stone Quarry Workers

On the lines of studies by Jan Breman (1996) and Tribhuwan Robin and Andreassen (2003) regarding the concept of social insecurity, facts regarding, health, insecurity, maternity benefits, nutritional insecurity, economic insecurity, civic amenities by quarry owners as well as Government is given below:

1. Health Insecurity

Out of total 150 respondents, it was observed that not a single respondent received following health security/facility:

- First aid treatment
- Special diet
- Medical aid from quarry company doctor
- Medical allowance
- Mediclaim policy

2. Maternity Benefits

Out of total 150 respondents interviewed, 100 per cent said that they do not receive any of the following maternity benefit during or after pregnancy for their wives from quarry owners.

- Calcium and iron tablets
- Nutritious food for pregnant women
- Medical Check-up
- Maternity leave
- Immunisation

3. Nutritional Insecurity

Out of 150 respondents, it was observed that no one have received any of the following nutritional security/facility from quarry owners:

- Nutrition supplement
- Canteen with subsidized rates
- Subsidised grocery

4. Economic Insecurity

Out of 150 respondents interviewed, 100 per cent of them said that there is no economic security provided to them by quarry owners.

— Provident fund

— Gratuity

— Pension

— Festival bonus

5. Civic Amenities

It was observed that, out of 150 respondents not a single respondent have received any of the following civic amenity:

— Regular water supply

— Electricity

— Public toilet and bathroom facility

— Drainage system

6. Benefits received from Government Schemes

It is surprising to note that out of 150 respondents not a single respondents have received the benefit of following Government Schemes:

—	I.C.D.S.	—	Ration Shop
—	Balwadi	—	Drinking water facility
—	Z.P. School	—	Housing Scheme
—	P.H.C.	—	Water tap
—	Sub-Centre	—	Educational Scholarship
—	Electricity	—	Others

Both qualitative and quantitative data on the stone quarry workers reveal that the owners of quarries do not provide economic, educational, nutritional, health and environmental securities including civic amenities to the degraded bread winners. It seems that the quarry owners employ poor, in secured workers whose native places are far away from the stone quarry sites.

CONCLUSIONS

Given below are few conclusions based on empirical data on the stone quarry communities storied:

(i) Poverty, illiteracy and lack of awareness about health leads to undernourishment among stone quarry worker women;

(ii) High incidences of respiratory disorders among stone-quarry workers are due to dust particles released by stone-crushers;

(iii) Incidences of digestive disorders among stone-quarry workers due to unavailability of pure, safe and clean drinking water;

(iv) Illiteracy, poverty, lack of labourer's unions, professional skills, leadership awareness about human rights and nomadic and insecured life leads to social, physical, educational and economical exploitation of the stone-quarry workers;

(v) Social, educational, economic, personal, health, nutritional, housing and civic insecurities among the labourers of unorganized sectors, are factors that one responsible for promoting the dependency of the labourers on the owners of unorganized firms;

(vi) Continuous education, training, awareness empowerment and financial assistance for higher education to the present generation of children attending "*Pashan Schools*" will psychologically prepare them to come out of the vicious circle of bonded labour;

(vii) Intervention of dedicated NGOs, Corporation Social Activists, Media Personnel and Committed Government Officers amongst stone quarry

communications and settlements can kindly their hopes of livelihood help them to live as dignified citizen of India.

RECOMMENDATIONS

This study has revealed that the stone quarry workers depend on their employers for their livelihood, despite of any social security provided to them. As citizens of a democratic country they deserve to live a dignified life, to be empowered and avail basic necessities and amenities of survival as per the Indian constitution. The recommendations given below will certainly help the policy makers and administrators of concerned Government Departments to give justice to the stone quarry workers.

1. Minimum Wages Norms

The stone quarry owners must be checked now and then to see if the Governments minimum wages norms for men and women are given to the labourers.

NGOs and the Media too have a role to play in this regard. They must boldly come forward and expose those stone quarry workers who are not abiding by the Governments minimum daily wage norms.

2. Civic Amenities

Although some stone quarry owners provide free housing to few workers, majority of them are deprived of this facility. It is recommended that basic amenities and facilities such as house, toilets, bathrooms, urinals, water tanks for washing clothes, drinking water facilities, electricity etc. should be provided by the owners for the labourer.

3. Health and First-aid Facilities

Basic facilities such as first-aid box with medicines, a mobile clinic in camp equipped with at least a Doctor, an A.N.M. and a driver-cum-compounder should be there in every quarry. The expenses of the same could be shared by all the owners. The A.N.M. can advice pregnant and lactating mothers. She can also assist in conducting safe deliveries. These basic facilities and amenities must be provided by quarry owners.

The local Municipal Corporations, Primary Health Centers and Government Medical Colleges can provide weekly medical services to the stone quarry labourers by going at the sites. Besides this NGOs working in the field of public health can take-up several programmes for stone quarry workers such as:

- Health check-up camps;
- Eye check-up camps;
- Treatment of minor illness;
- Provision of first-aid kits;
- Health and Nutrition education programmes;
- Preparation of IEC material;
- Nutrition supplement programmes;
- A.N.C. camps;
- Genetic counseling programmes;
- Government Health education programme;
- Health Insurance;
- Mediclaim, Accident, Death Compensation, Maternity and Medical Benefit, Policy Awareness Camps;
- Training of traditional midwives in the stone quarry camps;
- Providing the stone-quarry workers with hand-gloves, ear-muffs, shoes, glasses, helmets, caps etc. for their safety;
- Training to the labourers on preventive and promotive health-care practices;
- Creating awareness about boiling water before drinking it.

4. Economic Security

The stone quarry owners should be pressurised by both Government and NGOs to provide economic securities such as housing, provident fund, basic amenities, accident and injury claims, pension plans, festival bonus and more importantly job security as per the Government norms, to the workers.

5. Educational Security

An NGO by the name 'Santulan' is implementing educational programmes for the children of stone quarry workers under a banner called '*Pashan-Shala*'. The NGO is certainly doing well. The programme is being supported by the Government. It is recommended that more can be done in this field to promote assistance to stone quarry worker's children for higher education.

Through the '*Pashan-Shala*' programme several educational programmes can be promoted so as to motivate the children to develop confidence in them. Some of the programmes recommended for *Pashan-school* children, especially those ones in VIIIth, IXth and Xth grades are:

(i) Communication skills training programme;

(ii) Computer skills;

(iii) Personality development;

(iv) Career guidance workshops;

(v) Coaching classes for subjects like Mathematics, Science and English;

(vi) Exposure visits to institutions that train youth for MPSC, UPSC and other competitive exams;

(vii) Talent search and competition programmes among the *Pashan-school* students;

(viii) Human Right Issues;

(ix) Age at marriage and small family norms;

(x) Significance of documents such as ration card, election card, birth, marriage and death certificates etc.

(xi) Government programmes for stone quarry workers, scheduled castes, scheduled tribes, nomadic groups and other backward classes.

(xii) Constitutional provisions for SCs, STs and OBCs.

(xiii) *Libraries in 'Pashan-Shalas'*: Efforts should be made to promote small libraries in *Pashan-schools* so that the children have access to story, fiction, science, biographies and other important books. This will certainly help them to mature educationally;

(xiv) *Educational Posters:* The *Pashan-schools* should be equipped with posters that can educate them on health, hygiene discipline, manners etc.

(xv) *School Building:* It was observed that the *Pashan-Schools* are held in rooms made up of tins with exceptions of brick walled schools. It is recommended that the *Pashan-school* building should be strong of built with good material. The school buildings, in fact, should be planned as per Government norms, so that justice is given to the children. Government can outsource this kind of projects to NGOs like *'Santulan'*.

Further Research Needed

Since the topic researched by us has multidimensional and inter-disciplinary implications we felt that not only Sociologists but research scholars of other disciplines of social science such as Anthropology, Social Work, Economics, Political Science and Development Planning can conduct research on various aspects of life and development of labourers in the unorganised sector. One of the reasons of lack of empowerment and awareness among the stone quarry workers and other labourers is due to lack of involvement of social scientists in planning, implementing, monitoring and following up of development programmes, for this section (unorganised sector) of the society.

Hence, we strongly recommend that there is an urgent need to carry out inter-disciplinary research from a holistic perspective in the field of unorganised sector. This database will certainly be useful to the policy-makers and administrators to develop appropriate and culturally acceptable development programmes for the labourers of unorganised sectors. Given below are some of the areas of research that can be taken by social scientists as well as health and medical scientists:

(i) Baseline Survey

(a) Drinking water facilities in stone-quarries;

(b) Maternal morbidity and mortality among stone-quarry workers;

(c) Infant and child morbidity and mortality;

(d) A survey of health, nutritional and civic facilities and amenities at the stone-quarries in India;

(e) Nutritional status of children and women among the stone-quarry workers;

(f) Survey of awareness of Government Programmes among the stone-quarry workers.

(ii) Research Studies

(a) Legal issues of stone quarry workers

(b) Health beliefs and practices among stone quarry workers;

(c) Health seeking behaviour;

(d) Health insecurity among the labourers of unorganised sector;

(e) Insecurity issues and unorganised sector;

(f) Alcoholism and addiction behaviour among stone quarry workers;

(g) Types and processes of migration among the stone quarry workers;

(h) Impact of new economic policy on the lives of labourers of unorganised sector;

(i) Impact of technology on the livelihood and survival of stone quarry workers;

(j) Social and physical audit studies of stone-quarry owners.

(iii) Evaluation Research

(a) Impact of '*Pashanshala*' Programme on the lives of stone quarry workers children.

(b) Impact of social activism by NGOs on the socio-economic lives of stone-quarry workers.

(c) An evaluation of Government Programmes on the socio-economic lives of stone-quarry workers.

Although the above areas have been suggested for research, survey and evaluation studies to be conducted on stone quarry workers, the same framework applies to other labourers such as brick-kiln workers, sugarcane cutters etc.

REFERENCES

1. Breman Jan. 1996, *Footloose Labour—Working in India's Informal Economy*, Cambridge University Press, Cambridge.
2. Jhabvala Renana and Subrahmanya R.K.A., (eds) 2000, *The Unorganised Sector—Work Security and Social Protection*, Sage Publication.
3. Tribhuwan Robin and Andreassen Ragrihild, 2003, *Streets of Insecurity, A Study of Pavement Dwellers in India*, Discovery Publishing House, New Delhi.
4. Ginneken Wouter Van (ed.) 1998, *Social Security for All Indians*, Oxford Univcrsity Press, New Delhi.
5. Ahmad, Dreze A., Hills J. and Sen A. (eds.) 1990, *Social Security in Developing Countries*, Oxford University Press, New Delhi.
6. Singha Roy Debal K. (ed.) 2001, *Social Development and the Empowerment of Marginalised Groups: Perspectives and Strategies*, Sage Publication.
7. Chandra Ramesh (Ed.), 2004, *Social Development in India*, Isha Books, Delhi.
8. Tribhuwan Robin, 2004, *Health of Primitive Tribes*, Discovery Publishing House, New Delhi.
9. Jain Navinchandra and Tribhuwan Robin, 1996, *Mirage of Health and Development*, Vidya Nidhi Prakashan, Pune.
10. Singh K.S., 1993, *The Scheduled Castes, People of India Series*, Vol.II, Oxford University Press, New Delhi.

11. Crooke W., 1974, *Tribes and Castes of the North-western India*, Vol. I, Cosmo Publications, Delhi.
12. Russell R.V. and Hiralal, 1975, *Tribes and Castes of the Central Provinces of India*, Vol. II, Cosmo Publications, Delhi.
13. Sachidanand and Prasad R.R. 1996, *Encyclopaedic Profile of Indian Tribes*, Discovery Publishing House, New Delhi.
14. Naik D.B, *Labanis of Karnataka (A Cultural Study) South Central Zone Cultural Centre*, Nagpur.
15. Ketkar S.V., 1926, *Maharashtriya Dnyankosh (Sharirkhand)*, Maharashtriya Dnyankosh Mandal Limited, Nagpur.
16. Pt. Joshi Mahadevshastri (ed.), *Bhartiya Sanskrutikosh*, Vol. VIII, Bhartiya Sanskrutikosh Mandal, Pune.
17. Pt. Joshi Mahadevshastri (ed.), *Bhartiya Sanskrutikosh*, Vol. VI, Bhartiya Sanskrutikosh Mandal, Pune.
18. Chavan Ramnath Namdev, ... *Jati Ani Jamati* (Marathi Version) Mehta Publishing House, Pune.
19. Kamble Uttam, *Bhatkyanche Lagna* (Marathi Version).
20. Mande Prabhakar, ... *Gavachya Baher* (Marathi Version).
21. *Social Security for Unorganised Workers—A Report*, May 2006, National Commission for Enterprises in the Unorganised Sector, New Delhi.
22. Surjit Singh, 1994, *Urban Informal Sector,* Rawat Publications, Delhi.
23. Mane Laxman, 2007, *Vimuktayan, — Maharashtratil Vimukta Jamati : Ek Chikitsak Abhyas*, Yashawantrao Chavan Pratishthan, Mumbai
24. Joshi Shubhangi,1992, *Nutrition and Dieletics,* Tata McGraw-Hill Publishing Comapany Ltd. New Delhi.
25. Bhatia Arun and Tribhuwan Robin, 2002, '*Malnutrition Related Deaths of Tribal Children in Nandurbar*', A Report.
26. *Estimated Population of VJNT in Maharashtra*, ARTI, Pune (1999).

Index

A

Accidents, 166,
    place of treatment, 168
Analyses, 20
Availability of documents, 199

B

Beldars, 94-98
    clans, 95
    dress pattern, 95
    economic background, 98
    family pattern, 96
    festivals, 98
    food habits, 96
    geographical distribution, 94
    house types, 96
    language, 95
    marriage pattern, 96
    origin, 94
    population, 94
    religious practices, 97
    settlement pattern, 96
    subcastes, 94
    traditional occupation, 95
Borrowing behaviour, 161
Breman, Jan, 11, 12-14, 21

C

Caste categories, 26-27
Chavan, 35
Children in quarry, 27
Civic amenities, 198, 226
Constitution, 6

D

Definitions, 3
Degradation in the labour process, 14
Division of labour, 13

E

Economic assets, 160
Economic insecurity, 197, 226
Economic status, 158, 220-222
    annual income, 158-159
    job status, 160
    landholders, 159
    landless, 159
    possession of livestock, 159
Economist on security, 7
Economists on ILO, 7
Educational insecurity, 203
Educational status, 157, 218
Environmental issues, 190
    housing environment, 192
    hygiene, 193
    impact of pollution, 190-191
    water consumption, 192
    water scarcity, 193
Environmental problems, 194
Exploitation, 12

F

Family as a working unit, 12

G

Getubig, I.P., 3
Government schemes, 198, 226

H

Health, 222
Health insecurity, 195, 225
Health issues, 164-177
    deaths, 176
    family planning, 173-175
    habits, 175-176
    personnel conducting deliveries, 169
    place of deliveries of women, 169
    status of abortion, 173
Health policy, 162-164
    critique of NHP, 163
    introduction, 162
    national health policy, 163
Health problems, 194
Hirway, Indira, 4

I

ILO, 2, 3, 5
Inhuman work environment, 14
Injuries, 167
IT sector, 1

L

Lamans, 33-85
    anecdotes, 74
    ballad, 77
        historical ballad, 78
        mythological ballad, 78
        religious ballads, 78
    black magic, 60
    clans, 41
    cosmic nature, 35
    death rituals, 55-57
    descents of Wali and Sugreeva, 34
    dialect, 43-44
    dressing pattern, 42-43
    economic background, 81-85
    evil eye, 62
    family deities, 58
    family pattern, 46
    festivals, 63-68
    fire worship, 58
    folk songs, 76
    – tales, 75
    – tradition, 68
        art of embroidery, 71
        – – tattooing, 72
        dance, 68-71
        folk dramas, 72
        – music instruments, 72
        literature, 73
    geographical distribution, 33
    haveli song, 76
    historical evidences, 34-37
    house types, 46
    language, 43
    marriage
        religious worshipping, 57
        wadayi ceremony, 53
    – of divorced, 48
    – pattern, 47, 53-55
    – with brother's wife, 48
    medical system, 80-81
    method of singing, 77
    mythological evidences, 34-37
    mythologies, 73
    offering prey, 58
    origin, 33

polygamy, 48
population, 33
progeny, 35
proverbs, 78
religious rituals, 49
birth rites, 49
jalawa dhokayero, 50-51
mensuration, 52-53
tonsuration ceremony, 51-52
vekal peeyer, 50
riddles, 79
sati worship, 59
sorecery, 60
source of inscriptions, 40
sub-group, 41
traditional occupation, 44
food habits, 45
settlement pattern, 46
widow marriage, 47
women, 43
worshipping of ancestors, 60
– – shakati goddesses, 58-59
written evidence, 37
Legal provisions, 5
Living conditions, 27

M

Maharashtra, 25-26, 30
Marathas, 38, 81
Marx, Karl, 10
Maternity benefits, 225
Maternity insecurity, 195
Method of extracting stones, 12
Migration workers, 27
Miserable working conditions, 15-17
food intake, 16
illegally distilled alcohol, 16
job security, 17
medical care, 17
physical and mental agony, 17
sexual harassment, 16
women and hard workers, 16

N

Number of earning members, 160
Nutrition insecurity, 196-197
Nutrition problems, 194
Nutritional insecurity, 225
Nutritional issues, 177-190
government nutritional programme, 188
high intake of carbohydrates, 188
malnutrition, 177-188
NGOs, 188

P

Paine, Thomas, 9
Pawar sect, 34, 35
Payment system, 13
Primary data, 30
Pune district, 30

R

Rathod, 35
Replacement of locals by migrant workers, 12
Right to work, 9
Road construction workers, 13
Robson, W.A., 4

S

Secondary data, 30
Sen Amartya, 19
Settlement pattern, 218
and house types, 157
Skilled and unskilled work, 160
Social insecurity, 195, 224
Social security, 2, 5

history in India, 8
in developing countries, 8
legal provisions, 9
salient features, 18-20
unorganized sectors, 9
Social status, 219
Socio-economic status, 101, 218
age range of Beldar respondents, 109
– – – Laman respondents, 108
– – – Tirumal respondents, 109
– – – Wadar respondents, 107
annual income of the family, 128-135
area of house, 149
asset possession, 144
borrowing status, 138-141
caste-wise break-up of respondents, 103
economic status, 122-128
educational status, 115-121
family size, 113-115
frequency of buying clothes, 142
marital status of Beldars, 111-112
– – – Lamans, 110-111
– – – Tirumals, 112
– – – Wadara, 110, 111
mother tongue, 112
ownership of house, 145-149
possession of livestock, 137-138
schooling status, 152-156
sex-wise break-up of
Laman respondents, 105
respondents, 104
Tirumals respondents, 106-107
Wadar respondents, 105, 106
status of landholding, 135-137
Sociual status, 158
Sosial insurance schemes, 6
Subrahmanya, R.K.A., 10
Supervision by contractor's agents, 12

T

Technological changes, 13
Tirumals, 98-100
changes, 100
dialect, 98
family tupes, 99
festivals, 99
forms of marriage, 99
geographical distribution, 99
house type, 100
introduction, 98
origin, 98
religion, 99
settlement pattern, 99
traditional occupation, 99

U

Unorganized sectors, 9, 22
Unorganized sectors: characterised labour, 22-25

W

Wadars, 85-95
birth rituals, 92
clans, 87
death, 92
dressing pattern, 88
economic condition, 93
family apttern, 90
festivals, 93
folk traditions, 93
food habit, 89
house type, 90
language, 88

marriage pattern, 91-92
population, 85
religious practices, 92
settlement, 90
tattooing, 93
traditional occupation, 88-89
Weekly payment, 160

❑❑❑